T0315189

Praise for *Erasing History*

"*Erasing History* is both sequel and prequel to Jason Stanley's invaluable *How Fascism Works*, a sweeping survey of this global fascist moment's anti-education tide. From India to Turkey, from Russia to Florida—and maybe soon in a classroom near you—gross declarations of supremacist nationalism are becoming awful substitutes for historical inquiry. *Erasing History*, fast-paced and up-to-the-minute, tells us how it's happening and why the past is a front line in the struggle for a future free of fascism."

—Jeff Sharlet, *New York Times* bestselling author
of *The Undertow: Scenes from a Slow Civil War*

"Jason Stanley has been the essential voice for anyone seeking an unflinching account of the fascist dimensions of the current moment. In his latest contribution, Stanley turns his attention to the fascist attacks on institutions—in this case, schools and universities. *Erasing History* delivers a vital decoding of the wide-ranging effort of a small but well-organized and well-resourced faction seeking to consolidate power by censoring knowledge and rewriting the past. Their efforts to undermine faith in education weakens the role of institutions that have served as laboratories for democracy. Stanley has provided a clear-eyed account of how the survival of our democracy must be routed through a deepened literacy about our past and the myriad efforts to mystify and deny it."

—Kimberlé Crenshaw, cofounder and executive director of the
African American Policy Forum and coeditor of *Critical Race Theory*

"I've never read a book that is as timely, urgent, and essential as this one. *Erasing History* is, at this moment, the only source of knowledge I know of that is a sort of battle plan for keeping this nation from falling into fascism. You must read this book."

—Khalil Gibran Muhammad, author of *The Condemnation
of Blackness* and professor of African American Studies
and Public Affairs at Princeton University

ALSO BY JASON STANLEY

How Fascism Works
How Propaganda Works
The Politics of Language (with David Beaver)
Know How
Language in Context
Knowledge and Practical Interests

ERASING HISTORY

HOW FASCISTS REWRITE THE PAST TO CONTROL THE FUTURE

JASON STANLEY

ONE SIGNAL
PUBLISHERS

ATRIA

New York London Toronto Sydney New Delhi

ONE SIGNAL
PUBLISHERS

ATRIA

An Imprint of Simon & Schuster, LLC
1230 Avenue of the Americas
New York, NY 10020

First One Signal Publishers/Atria Books hardcover edition September 2024

ONE SIGNAL PUBLISHERS / ATRIA BOOKS
and colophon are trademarks of Simon & Schuster, LLC

Simon & Schuster: Celebrating 100 Years of Publishing in 2024

For information about special discounts for bulk purchases, please contact Simon & Schuster Special Sales at 1-866-506-1949 or business@simonandschuster.com.

The Simon & Schuster Speakers Bureau can bring authors to your live event. For more information, or to book an event, contact the Simon & Schuster Speakers Bureau at 1-866-248-3049 or visit our website at www.simonspeakers.com.

Interior design by Davina Mock-Maniscalco

Manufactured in the United States of America

7   9   10   8   6

Library of Congress Cataloging-in-Publication Data has been applied for.

ISBN 978-1-6680-5691-2
ISBN 978-1-6680-5693-6 (ebook)

To my children, Emile and Alain

CONTENTS

Preface   xi

1. How to Create an Autocracy   1

2. Colonizing the Mind   25

3. The Nationalist Project   45

4. From Supremacism to Fascism   75

5. Anti-education   111

6. Classical Education   135

7. Reclaiming History   161

Epilogue   185

Acknowledgments   191

Notes   197

Index   219

PREFACE

> The Soviet system never commemorated the Holocaust. One reason for this is that once you define and identify one genocide, you can recognize other genocidal crimes. The Soviet empire didn't want us to learn our history.
>
> —Victoria Amelina, "Nothing Bad Has Ever Happened"[1]

One lesson the past century has taught us is that authoritarian regimes often find history profoundly threatening. At every opportunity, these regimes find ways of erasing or concealing history in order to consolidate their power. Why is this? What does history do that is so disruptive of authoritarian goals? Perhaps most importantly, it provides multiple perspectives on the past. Authoritarianism's great rival, democracy, requires the recognition of a shared reality that consists of multiple perspectives. Through exposure to multiple perspectives, citizens learn to regard one another as equal contributors to a national narrative. And they learn, *we* learn, to accept that this narrative is open to continued collective reflection and re-imagination, constantly taking into account new ideas, new evidence, new perspectives and theoretical framings. History in a democracy is not static, not mythic, but dynamic and critical.

Erasing history helps authoritarians because doing so allows them to misrepresent it as a single story, a single perspective. But it is impossible to erase a perspective entirely. When authoritarians attempt to erase history, they do so through education, by purging certain narratives from the curricula taught in schools, and perhaps by forbidding their telling at home. However, authoritarians cannot erase people's lived experiences, and their legacies written into the bones of generations. In this simple fact lies always the possibility of reclaiming lost perspectives.

All of this is true of authoritarianism generally, but it is especially true of one specific kind of authoritarian ideology: fascism, which seeks to divide populations into "us" and "them" by appealing to ethnic, racial, or religious differences. In my previous book *How Fascism Works: The Politics of Us and Them*, I identified a set of tactics that characterize fascist politics, which include: the creation of a mythic past; the use of propaganda and anti-intellectualism to create a state of unreality; an effort to justify hierarchies of race or religion; the exploitation of feelings of resentment and victimhood; policies that prioritize law and order over freedom; appeals to sexual anxiety; an evocation of the myth of Sodom and Gomorrah, which holds that cities are decadent and crime ridden, and that rural areas are the heartland of a nation; and finally, a value system that ranks groups according to their supposed capacity to work, encapsulated by the slogan the Nazis hypocritically used, *Arbeit macht frei*, or work shall make you free.[2]

The rise of contemporary fascism poses a grave threat and makes urgent the task of understanding its workings. Truly understanding fascism's success, however, requires discerning not just how it operates and seizes power but also how it achieves legitimacy. We must therefore turn the lens from fascist politics to the kind of education and culture that makes such a politics effective. This is where the topic of erasing history looms large.

In recent years, a debate has broken out among scholars and pundits about whether the term "fascism" appropriately describes the ascendant right-wing authoritarian movements we are seeing around the world. We can largely bypass this debate here. Whether we call them fascist or not, there is widespread agreement that the social and political movements we are witnessing today employ many of the same political tactics and rhetorical techniques that past fascist movements have—conjuring violent vigilante mobs to threaten those who oppose them, stacking courts with loyalists to a leader or a party, directing hatred against immigrants and LGBTQ citizens, dismantling reproductive rights, and using education to indoctrinate the young in a narrative of national greatness, rooted in a glorious past.

While some may disagree with my decision to call these movements fascist—including some who share my assessment of the danger they pose—I find the label apt, and will continue to use it in these pages when referring to those who engage in clearly fascist politics, with the aim of attacking democracy.

Because these anti-democratic movements are ascendant throughout the world, my scope here is international and will cover, at various points, fascist or authoritarian cultures in countries such as Russia, India, Turkey, Israel, and Hungary. However, with that said, I live in the United States, and my country will serve as a central example. Here, as elsewhere, an ideological war has been taking place in recent years that extends into nearly every aspect of our culture. The fight dips into our neighborhoods, our courts, and our bedrooms but ultimately, as I will show, finds its deepest expression in one of our most egalitarian public institutions: our schools. The sides in this war have largely been shaped by two opposing perspectives: those who wish to preserve hierarchies rooted in arbitrary factors like race, ethnicity, and gender—and those who wish to upend them.

✦ ✦ ✦

My grandmother Ilse Stanley, born in 1906, was raised in Berlin, in the shadow of the Fasanenstrasse Synagogue, one of the largest congregations in Germany at the time, where her father, Magnus Davidsohn, was the chief Cantor. The Fasanenstrasse Synagogue practiced the German Jewish liberal tradition. Like a church, it had an organ. Its music was proudly in the classical tradition. My grandmother was the archetype of the assimilated German Jew, and as she saw it, German culture—the culture of Goethe and Heine—was her own. It was a beacon of enlightenment and humanism.

Before becoming a Cantor, Magnus Davidsohn was an opera singer. He is mentioned in a biography of the composer and conductor Gustav Mahler, which quotes from a conversation between the two about their shared Jewish heritage and my great-grandfather's decision to leave the opera for the synagogue.[3] At the time of that conversation, he was singing a central part in an 1899 production of Richard Wagner's *Lohengrin* that Mahler was conducting. His brother Max would later sing in the same opera, as part of the Bayreuth Festival in 1908.

Ilse, descended from this family of Wagner singers, became an actress and trained with the great Berlin theater director Max Reinhardt. She also acted for director Fritz Lang in his groundbreaking 1927 film, *Metropolis*.[4] She lived in one of the great intellectual and cultural capitals of the world, home to a renowned university, which hosted such luminaries as W. E. B. Du Bois, Albert Einstein, Max Planck, Erwin Schrödinger, and Max Weber.

Yet just a few years later, my German Jewish family in Berlin would be ejected from this cosmopolitan paradise. How could this be? How could it come to pass that my grandmother, whose talents had earned her a place of prominence within the German culture, would be banned from the theater, her artistry deemed dangerous and alien?

When the Nazis came to power in Germany, they placed at the ideological center of their political movement a fictional view of the country and its people: a land inhabited by a pure race of Aryans, which had been infiltrated by Jewish foreigners, who were seeking to undermine German institutions and topple the dominance of the German race.

At the heart of fascist ideology broadly, and Nazi ideology specifically, is this conspiracy about the replacement of a dominant group. The Nazis enacted laws that stripped German Jews of citizenship, casting them as a dangerous internal enemy, and took as their target the very cosmopolitanism that my grandmother exemplified. Her identification with German culture did little to protect her because it contradicted the Nazi narrative in which her role was predetermined and unchangeable. Her assimilation was not what the Nazis wanted, but precisely what they were trying to prevent. As the Nazis saw it, Germany's greatness was based not on its broad humanism and commitments to experimentation and . intellectual innovation, but on its Aryan character.

Germany in the 1920s had some of the best universities

in the world, many of the world's leading intellectuals, and was at the leading edge of modernity. For that reason, a study of the fascist sacking of Germany, and the ideology's successful mutation of the nation's self-conception, has much to tell us about the rising threats we face today. That nation's self-understanding of its history and identity, preserved through its schools and its culture, was proven to be far less protective than many believed. We would be wise to avoid the same misapprehension.

✦   ✦   ✦

For some, the United States' ethos of openness and freedom may seem incompatible with fascism's project of erasing history until it is reduced to a single perspective. But this impulse to eliminate historical narratives can have many different motivations, some of which may be more palatable than others. Consider the era of the Red Scare in the United States during the late 1940s and 1950s, often referred to as the McCarthy era after the red-hunting senator from Wisconsin. This was a time when leftists in higher education, the arts, and other fields were publicly humiliated, denounced by Congress, and fired from their jobs in sensational fashion. This campaign of censorship and intimidation, led by the House Un-American Activities Committee (HUAC), was principally concerned with hunting down communists, socialists, and anyone who might harbor sympathy for the country's adversary in the Cold War, the Soviet Union.

In this instance, the HUAC's effort to erase leftist perspectives from the academy and elsewhere was motivated, at least in part, by opposition to the Soviet Union's authoritarianism—which, of course, in no way excuses its destructive overreaches. The Red Scare of the 1940s and '50s was a betrayal of the very ideals of freedom that the United States purported to represent in the Cold War. However, the episode does at least partly explain how and why the fascist project of erasing history can take root in a distinctly American context.

Today we are unquestionably returning to something like the era of the Red Scare. Right-wing activists and politicians are targeting educators at all levels for their supposedly leftist ideologies, with the goal of suppressing any teaching that challenges racial hierarchy or patriarchy. But this assault on history goes far beyond local school boards, state departments of education, or even national elections. It is, in fact, a transnational movement with deep historical precedent. And it is symptomatic of a larger global attack on liberal democracy.

A liberal democracy is a system that centers the values of freedom and equality, in which all citizens have equal political value—and are thus entitled to equal respect and dignity. With that freedom comes responsibility, including the responsibility to safeguard and improve the institution of democracy. Progressive educational movements within liberal democracies have long served to draw out this sense of responsibility in young people.

Education, however, does not always serve this purpose—it can also be wielded against democracy and in service of hierarchy. And this is precisely where so many of the recent battles over education have been waged. In a liberal democracy, there will always be (and should always be) debates between different visions of how education should work—over questions such as the proper balance between the pursuit of secular ideals and the preservation of shared traditions, or whether to place greater emphasis on liberal or vocational education. But education can also support an anti-democratic agenda. In the cases of Russia and North Korea today, we can see how education systems help to cultivate an unhealthy reverence for leaders, placing them above the rule of law. In other countries, such as India, the education system is used to place Hindu Indians over Muslim Indians. In each case, education functions to undermine the basis of democratic equal citizenship.

To be clear, hierarchies are not inherently oppressive. In a medical school, for example, an attending physician stands in a hierarchy over medical students. This is an example of an epistemological hierarchy, one based on *knowledge*. Knowledge can certainly be employed to mask subjugation and control—a doctor can be directed to diagnose an anti-colonial rebel or a political protestor as mentally unstable—but ideally, at least, epistemological hierarchies guide rather than dominate. A hierarchy of value is different, serving to place one group of people above another or one individual over all others, and is typically used to justify the domination of certain groups or individuals. Hierarchies of value violate the fundamental ideals of liberal democracy—and, indeed, cannot tolerate the equal moral and political status of all people.

✦ ✦ ✦

Because this is a book about fascist culture, it is worth saying a bit more about what exactly cultures are and how they work. Taking up a proposition of the Swiss philosopher Rahel Jaeggi, we can think of a culture as *a form of life*—a coordinated web of practices, orientations, and myths.[5] Cultures of hierarchy—such as colonialism, nationalism, or fascism—involve practices that place one group above others. And as is the case with all other cultures, or forms of life, these practices are in large part shaped and reinforced by schools.

Every education system involves erasure—one simply cannot teach everything. There are, however, certain *kinds* of erasures that are constitutive of authoritarian systems. For example, erasures of social movements for democracy, such as the Chinese government's erasure of the Tiananmen Square protest and massacre of 1989, or the state of Florida's erasure of the 2020 Black Lives Matter uprisings from a social studies curriculum.[6] By removing the history of uprisings against the current status quo from the curriculum (or never allowing that history to be taught in the first place), authoritarians leave students with the impression that the status quo has never been—and cannot be—challenged.

1

How to Create an Autocracy

Wars are won by teachers.

—Vladimir Putin[1]

In a prescient 1995 address at Howard University titled "Racism and Fascism," the Pulitzer Prize–winning author Toni Morrison warned of forces within the United States "interested in fascist solutions to national problems."[2] These fascist solutions, she explained, involve both representations and practices—in other words, what fascists say or believe and what they do. As Morrison pointed out, representations and practices can be mutually reinforcing. Representations can make practices that would otherwise be unacceptable seem normal and justified, while practices can make representations seem retrospectively apt. The representation of immigrants as dangerous criminals justifies the practice of penning them in large prison-like centers; once they are there, the fact that they are imprisoned leads some to conclude that they must be dangerous.

To understand the power that fascism can wield in the

realm of education, it is first necessary to understand some of its representations and practices. According to the Nazi political theorist Carl Schmitt, "[t]he specific political distinction to which political actions and motives can be reduced is that between friend and enemy."[3] Which is to say, for fascists, being political means defining oneself against an enemy. As such, fascist regimes selectively disenfranchise certain segments of their population and violently cast them into what the political philosopher Elizabeth F. Cohen calls "semi-citizenship," in order to emphasize the virtue and worth of the dominant group.[4]

Fascist regimes are also typically organized around a charismatic leader—and form social and political cultures centered on that leader, who is taken to be the violent and powerful protector of the nation. Russia's Vladimir Putin is a clear contemporary example. All of Russia is centered around Putin's rule, and Putin is represented as the powerful male leader upon whose shoulders Russian greatness rests. But fascism can also be leaderless. The southern United States under the Jim Crow system of segregation, for example, was governed by a form of racial fascism premised not on a single powerful leader, but on decentralized groups of vigilantes and terrorists. To fully understand the imminent threat of fascism today, we must pay careful attention to fascist movements that are not necessarily based on reverence for the leader.

Regardless of how it is led, a fascist culture, or form of

life, often has certain features that make it an ideal environment for fascist politics. These cultures will, for instance, elevate an already dominant group of people to a mythic status, exalting them as "the people" who constitute the nation, while relegating others to second-class citizenship. From a fascist perspective, egalitarianism is a threat because it promises to upset this hierarchy. The threat is felt so acutely that fascists are led to take joy in cruelty against those outside this group, and others who stand to benefit from greater equality. A fascist form of life is suffused with fear that others will achieve equal status, a possibility cynically exploited in fascist politics.

A fascist form of life also has certain requirements. Perhaps most importantly, it requires an education system that can validate the dominant group's elevated status as a justified consequence of history rather than the fabricated result of intentional choices. It does this, as we will see, by selectively doctoring the historical record, erasing perspectives and events that are unflattering to the dominant group, and replacing them with a unitary, simplified account that supports its ideological ends.

In recent years, for example, the United States has seen a wave of right-wing political interference in education focused on banning certain concepts, authors, and books from schools' libraries and curricula. The unstated goal of these bans is to erase the perspectives and histories of marginalized groups, including most prominently the history of Black Americans, whose ancestors were enslaved and brutally subjugated in this country.

These bans target especially concepts and theories used to explain how that subjugation operated, how it has changed over time and persisted to this day, and how it might be challenged—concepts such as structural racism, intersectionality, and critical race theory (CRT). The concept of structural racism, for instance, is targeted because it explains racial subjugation not in terms of individual bigotry, but as a result of underlying systems and practices—whether in housing, schooling, banking, policing, or the criminal legal system. It explains, for example, that the racial wealth gap in America (which is so extreme that Black Americans possess just over 15 percent of white Americans' wealth) is a product of racist policies such as discriminatory lending and redlining. The concept of intersectionality, introduced by the law professor Kimberlé Crenshaw, reveals the particularly acute harms inflicted on groups that are at the intersection of multiple oppressions.[5]

Critical race theory is the study of these concepts, and emerged from the work of American legal theorists in the 1980s and 1990s, centrally including Harvard Law professor Derrick Bell, Northeastern professor Patricia J. Williams, and Professor Crenshaw. In the rhetoric of those who seek to ban it, the term "critical race theory" has morphed into something completely unrelated to its true meaning, and is imagined as something like a system for dividing groups into categories of oppressor and oppressed, the purpose of which is to saddle white people with a permanent and debilitating sense of guilt for the wrongdoing of their ancestors.

In erasing these concepts, or transforming them into meaningless slogans, the recent right-wing campaign of educational suppression seeks to eliminate an important means of understanding Black history. But critical race theory and Black history are impossible to separate. History is the study of not just people and events but also the practices, structures, and institutions that shape them. Without accounting for these forces, history is rendered flat and malleable—ideal for manipulation by fascist politics.

When fascists attempt to rewrite history, they sometimes claim that they are erasing only theories and interpretations of history, which they claim to be biased, rather than underlying historical events. But they know well that their interventions result in the erasure of events themselves, as well as the patterns they form. In her celebrated 2021 book, *America on Fire*, the historian Elizabeth Hinton identifies a recurring pattern in mid-twentieth-century US history that she calls "the cycle," in which over-policing and police violence elicit rebellions within the communities these practices affect. This pattern, she explains, "helped define urban life in segregated, low-income, Black, Mexican American, and Puerto Rican communities," and ultimately "put this nation on the path to mass incarceration."[6]

Hinton's thesis is based not in abstract theory, but in an account of the historical forces and events that led the United States to where it is today. Without this history, it is impossible to understand, for example, how and why the United States came to have the largest prison population of any country in the world. Hinton's work shows how institutions—from urban police to public housing and segregated, underfunded schools—have, through their practices, entrenched a racially unjust status quo. Ultimately, it is not possible to teach the history of what happened to Black Americans without teaching about structural racism. When these concepts are banned, the result is, in practice, to forbid schools from teaching any honest account of US history.

The Anti-Racist Teaching and Learning Collective (ARTLC) is an organization in Connecticut that brings together teachers, organizers, and students in order to, as the group's website puts it, "address the oppressive effects of the racism that shape public education and society at large." The website also includes a series of firsthand accounts from teachers of the practices they have employed in the classroom to help build a common understanding of structural racism.

Marco Cenabre, for example, teaches literature at New Haven Academy, a public high school in New Haven. In one of Cenabre's classroom lessons, the students are asked to study the Civics portion of the US naturalization test, as well as a classic essay from Audre Lorde that discusses "mythical norms" related to age, race, class, and sex.[7] What does the information an immigrant must learn about American history to become a naturalized American reveal about mythical norms? Does it elevate one group's history over others? Does it allow certain misconceptions to be normalized?

Ruth Terry Walden teaches literature at Westhill High School, a public school in Stamford, and focuses her courses on themes of protest, resistance, and direct action. In her classroom, she invites her students to think about why, during the Colonial era, the ordinary people began to see the British as an occupying army, and how that led to the American Revolution. She asks them to consider this in the context of the Black Lives Matter movement, as a way of understanding how Black residents of Ferguson, Missouri, may have come to regard the police as an occupying army.

Other teachers who are part of the ARTLC testify to the immense difficulty of teaching these sorts of lessons without support from school administrators. Samm Leska, a teacher at Staples High School, a public school in Westport, explains that her peers are reluctant to engage in such teaching practices, since they do not feel that the administration will support them if they become a target of political attacks for teaching on supposedly controversial topics. Since even noting the existence of structural racism is considered "critical race theory," all but the bravest teachers tend to avoid discussing texts that present students with Black perspectives on US history. This means that it takes a measure of bravery to teach the works of the Nobel Prize–winning Black American novelist Toni Morrison, even in states where that is legal.

It should be no surprise that right-wing politicians' efforts to stifle any discussion of structural racism extend naturally into a program of combating on-the-ground efforts to redress the harms of racism—and thwarting efforts to build a truly multi-racial democracy that is inclusive of all groups. One way that institutions in the United States have sought to address racism is through what are called Diversity, Equity, and Inclusion (DEI) initiatives. Predictably, these efforts are often targeted by the same right-wing forces that pour so much energy into attacking the history and theory of racism. The arguments are mutually reinforcing: if there is no racism, nothing needs to be done about it.

Broadly speaking, DEI initiatives are any programs at schools, universities, or private companies that seek to ameliorate the effects of structural racism in teaching, hiring, or institutional mission. For example, a DEI program at a medical school might seek to make sure that doctors from affluent white backgrounds are aware of the structural barriers that patients from other backgrounds may face. Such a program may, for instance, provide non-disabled doctors with insight into the barriers facing patients who are disabled.

As they do with CRT, the right-wing critics of DEI intentionally distort these programs to create the impression that those whose perspectives are finally being included—like Black Americans, for instance—are receiving some sort of illicit benefit or an unfair advantage. And so they target Black Americans who have risen to positions of power and influence and seek to delegitimize them as undeserving. The ultimate goal is to justify a takeover of the institutions, transforming them into weapons in the war against the very idea of multi-racial democracy.

✦ ✦ ✦

In the years since former US president Donald Trump's defeat in the 2020 election, and especially as he has waged his third campaign for office in 2023 and 2024, his fascist tendencies have only grown more extreme. He has, for instance, suggested suspending the Constitution's individual protections, called for drug dealers to be executed, mused about plans to prosecute his political rivals and investigate journalists for treason, said that some migrants are "not people," and promised a "blood bath" if he is not reelected.[8] His grip over his supporters takes the form of a classic cult of the leader. The Republican Party that he leads and the broader conservative movement have doubled down on their support for him, largely casting out any remaining "Never Trump" dissidents.

For these reasons, and others, the United States, at the time of this writing, is an excellent illustrative example to employ in theorizing contemporary fascist movements.

Project 2025, a blueprint for the potential second Trump administration is authored by a number of right-wing think tanks and other partners, including the Heritage Foundation. The nearly nine-hundred-page document lays out a plan to avoid the chaos and disorder that kept Trump from achieving his most extreme ambitions during his first term. According to a report from *The Guardian*, the plan calls for "changing federal service rules that would allow Trump to cut tens of thousands of civil service workers and replace them with ones deemed loyal to Trump's agenda."[9] The mass replacement of bureaucrats and government officials by those loyal to the leader is a prominent feature of fascist takeovers. In 1930s Germany, during the first years of Hitler's rule, the process of this kind of replacement played so important a role that a special name was coined for it, *Gleichschaltung*, which is often translated as "coordination."

Trump himself has been explicit about his plans for K-12 and (if possible) university education, branded as the"war on woke," some version of which seems almost essential to the fascist moment worldwide (as we shall see in detail in the pages to come). Branded as a strategy to "Save American Education and Give Power Back to Parents," Trump's plan will:

+ "Cut federal funding for any school or program pushing critical race theory, gender ideology or other inappropriate racial, sexual or political content on our children"

+ "Create a new credentialing body to certify teachers who embrace patriotic values, and understand that their job is not to indoctrinate children, but to educate them"

+ "Find and remove the radicals, zealots and Marxists who have infiltrated the federal Department of Education"

+ "Keep men out of women's sports" (By which the plan means banning transgender students who identify as girls from participating in sports.)[10]

It is no accident that an explicitly authoritarian campaign chose to foreground this plan. Fascist movements center education as a means of erasing concepts and histories that stand in the way of fascist goals.

Many of the strategies and goals of Trump's education plan are already being tested in states with conservative leadership. Nowhere is this more evident than in Florida, where legislators have enacted sweeping changes within the higher education system. According to a special report by the American Association of University Professors (AAUP) in December 2023, "the political interference in classroom teaching that began in 2021 is unprecedented in its sweep and ambition in both the state and the nation, with a frightening potential impact on the academic freedom of faculty members."[11] The state of Florida is an example, in the United States, of what we might call educational authoritarianism, a strategy in which politicians restrict the knowledge that educators can convey, with the goal of intimidating them into spreading an antidemocratic ideology.

✦ ✦ ✦

Educational authoritarianism is frequently accompanied by more general restrictions on knowledge, and by attempts to push mythic representations in place of that knowledge. Nazi education, for example, stressed the myth that Jews and communists had betrayed Germany in World War I. Of course, this myth was accompanied by other authoritarian and anti-Semitic practices, including the restriction of Jews from participating in the workplace and the imprisonment of anyone the Nazis deemed "Marxists."

The Nazis infamously maintained strict control over the publication and dissemination of books. The Nazi propaganda minister, Joseph Goebbels, kept lists of books to be censored on the grounds that they were "alien" or "decadent."[12] Today many activist groups in the United States are also seeking to constrain the free flow of books and ideas, even beyond school walls—by restricting, for instance, the offerings of local public libraries. As Deborah Caldwell-Stone of the American Library Association explained to the *New York Times* in 2023, "A year, a year and a half ago, we were told that these books didn't belong in school libraries, and if people wanted to read them, they could go to a public library. . . . Now, we're seeing those same groups come to public libraries and come after the same books, essentially depriving everyone of the ability to make the choice to read them."[13]

Because educational authoritarianism serves to bolster already dominant groups, in the twentieth and twenty-first centuries it has frequently been used to target LGBTQ people, labeling them as somehow inherently decadent or obscene. Russia under Vladimir Putin provides a clear example. In 2013, Russia passed what became known as the "gay propaganda law," which banned the distribution of materials containing any positive or even neutral representations of non-heterosexual relationships to anyone under the age of eighteen. In 2022, Putin signed legislation expanding the scope of that law, making it illegal for anyone to publicly suggest that queer relationships are normal, even to adults.[14] And considerably less extreme laws that cast LGBTQ identity as problematic are an increasingly common feature of authoritarian regimes in other countries as well.

Throughout the world, fascist propagandists reserve some of their foulest attacks for the trans community, which they claim is advancing a vaguely defined "gender ideology." Putin, for example, has justified Russia's 2022 invasion of Ukraine, in part, by arguing that it is fighting against such an ideology. In a ceremony in the Kremlin to announce the annexation of four Ukrainian regions, Putin set up the war in Ukraine as an existential conflict of values between a decadent West and Russia's defense of traditional gender roles:

> . . . do we want to have, here, in our country, in Russia, parent number one, number two, number three instead of mom and dad—have they gone mad out there? Do we really want perversions that lead to degradation and extinction to be imposed on children in our schools from the primary grades? To be drummed into them that there are various supposed genders besides women and men, and to be offered a sex change operation? Do we want all this for our country and our children? For us, all this is unacceptable, we have a different future, our own future.[15]

In the United States, the attack on trans rights has become unrelenting as the conservative movement has seized upon the issue to galvanize their base. According to a report by attorney and writer Heron Greenesmith, by the end of 2023 nearly half of the US states, a total of twenty-two, had "passed bans on gender-affirming medical or surgical care for transgender and nonbinary minors"—some of which were held up by court challenges, though many had taken effect. In five of these states, to give gender-affirming medical help to a minor is a felony. In my state of Connecticut, a trans student would be acclimated to using the restroom of their choice. It would be difficult for their parents to consider moving to any of the nine states in which that is illegal. In fact, it would be difficult for families living in trans-accepting states to move to any of these twenty-two states.[16] If such bans are national, families with trans children who have the means to do so will have to consider leaving the United States.

✦ ✦ ✦

Fascist attacks on LGBTQ people are part of a broader effort to diminish or eliminate what are regarded as "alien" perspectives. This is true of education systems not just in the United States and Russia but throughout the world.

Let's illustrate this with an example we will discuss a great deal in this book, the case of Hungary. Under its autocratic prime minister Viktor Orbán, Hungary introduced in early 2020 a new National Core Curriculum. The curriculum presents Hungarian literature as the literature of ethnic Hungarian populations, even those living outside of the borders of the state of Hungary after the Treaty of Trianon created Hungary in 1920. The course includes thematic studies of topics likes "Trianon in Hungarian literature." It excludes the work of Imre Kertész, Hungary's only Nobel Prize winner for literature, surrendering a national point of pride in order to erase the contributions of a Jewish survivor of the Holocaust.[17] And it adds to the core curriculum Ferenc Herczeg, a minor ring-wing nationalist playwright who was celebrated and praised by Miklós Horthy, the World War II Hungarian leader who brought Hungary into an alliance with Nazi Germany, and elevated to a national hero.[18] Previous revisions of the core curriculum in prior Orbán administrations had already elevated similar minor writers into the pantheon on an obvious political basis, such as József Nyírő, a member of Parliament for the fascist Hungarian Arrow Cross Party with a passionate hatred of Jews.[19] The new curriculum presents past far-right Hungarian nationalist leaders as heroes, minimizing or entirely omitting their support for anti-Semitic legislation and practices.

In May 2022, Orbán reorganized his administration to place education under the jurisdiction of the Ministry of the Interior, which is responsible for maintaining order through law enforcement.[20] A few months later—shortly after declaring that Hungary would not become a "mixed-race" country— Orbán was featured as a main speaker at the Conservative Political Action Conference (CPAC) in Dallas, Texas, where he was greeted by American conservatives with a standing ovation. In March 2024, Orbán visited the Heritage Foundation for a private event. The next day, he was feted by Trump at his Mar-a-Lago home.

In 2009, I had the opportunity to spend a summer in

Hungary, where I was co-directing a summer school program at Central European University (CEU) in Budapest. More than fifty faculty and students from all over the world gathered in that beautiful city. At the time, CEU, which had been established less than two decades earlier, in 1991, was quickly earning a reputation as an important center of international research in multiple fields. An emerging great university, it sat in the heart of a great European city, with a vibrant, cosmopolitan feel. Hungarian intellectuals assured me that the country was in the process of returning to its former status as a cultural center, and that the university's presence in the heart of Budapest was only natural, a reminder of Hungary's immense intellectual legacy and bright future.

When I returned the next year, in the summer of 2010, the mood in Hungary had changed dramatically. I could see it among not only the Budapest intellectuals I knew but the university's international faculty as well. Viktor Orbán had come to power by stoking a wave of resentment over many of the issues that ascendant fascists commonly exploit, including, in the case of Hungary, the significant loss of land it had suffered nearly a century earlier, at the end of World War I, under the Treaty of Trianon. He blamed this failure to establish "Greater Hungary" on leftist ideology spread by intellectuals, and vilified Central European University in particular as a source of this supposedly anti-Hungarian ideology. Orbán's campaign also attacked as false the only recently emerged consensus that many nationalist figures from Hungary's history had been complicit with fascism during World War II, if not active participants. The negative reputation of Hungarian nationalism for its connections to Nazism, though well established in the historical record, was dismissed as a smear. The campaign was a great success, drawing support from broad constituencies.

I was, at the time, much more pessimistic than my Hungarian friends, who responded to Orbán's tactics with resignation. "It's just national politics," they said. My friends on the CEU faculty also found it easy to dismiss the political upheaval as overblown—they taught at a great university in a cosmopolitan city. Their children were receiving good educations for free in Hungarian public schools.

Nearly a decade later, in 2019, I returned to Budapest once more, to give Central European University's annual opening week lecture. The difference couldn't have been starker. In the intervening years, Orbán had revoked CEU's accreditation, which meant that Hungary's best university would soon have to move out of the country, and it had already begun that process. Some of my Hungarian friends in Budapest now complained about the terrible state of the public schools and particularly the blatant nationalist nonsense their children were forced to absorb.

In the United States today, a similar situation has begun to unfold, as right-wing activists and politicians launch attacks on non-religious universities—and the public education system in general—that mirror Orbán's in Hungary. As is often the case with fascist rhetoric, their arguments are opportunistic and inconsistent, condemning universities both for restricting free speech (in the case of their allies) and for allowing too much free speech (in the case of their adversaries). Opportunism in rhetoric is an effective political strategy. Since 2015, when the conservative movement began to make education a central theme of its propaganda, ramping up the frequency and intensity of these attacks, they have managed to steadily chip away at Americans' confidence in higher education. The effect is most pronounced among Republicans. According to surveys conducted by Gallup, the portion of Republicans with confidence in higher education dropped by 17 percentage points between 2015 and 2018, and by another 20 points between 2018 and 2023, reaching a low of 19 percent.[21]

In many cases, the leaders of the fight targeting public education are also working to expand religious education—and to blur the lines between the two. Florida governor Ron DeSantis, for instance, instituted a new teacher-training initiative within the state's public schools that brought teachers to workshops developed in conjunction with Hillsdale College, a far-right Christian college in Michigan that has played a prominent role in the so-called culture wars. During one session, according to some of the teachers who attended, facilitators minimized the role that slavery played in the United States, and explained that the country's founders were opposed to a strict separation of church and state. The teachers described the program as having a "Christian fundamentalist" or Christian nationalist slant.[22]

The blurring of public and religious education is of course a long-standing goal of the conservative movement, and has included efforts to allow prayer in public schools, place creationist teachings alongside lessons on evolution, and steer tax dollars to private religious schools in the form of vouchers. All of this lays bare the hypocrisy of conservative efforts to remove ideology from government-funded education. DeSantis and his advisors, it seems, would have us believe that workshops involving Hillsdale College are non-ideological. In spite of the blatant hypocrisy, however, this line of attack is effective, both here and abroad.

During the writing of this book, the Palestinian political and military organization Hamas carried out a brutal terrorist attack against Israel, which prompted Israel to retaliate with an arguably genocidal campaign of mass killing in Gaza, the Palestinian territory that Hamas oversees. Immediately, some right-wing commentators in the United States were intent on connecting the conflict (in a bizarre leap of logic) to the supposed depravity of the US education system, singling out universities and their administrators for special attack. Months before coordinated anti-war protests grew on American campuses, in an October 16 broadcast, Fox News host Greg Gutfeld drew an analogy between Hamas's terrorist attack on Israel and the negative effects that he imagines universities to have had on the United States. As Gutfeld explained,

> The left has dehumanized Americans to a point where crime is now our punishment. Our universities have become lunatic incubators, which the federal government funds. They should try registering for women's studies in the Middle East, if you can get permission from your husband. And so the difference between Israel and the US, is really a matter of degrees. The attack on Israel is a deep fry versus our slow boil. The heat source is the same. The idea of lineage shaming, which means you had it coming. Sit there and take it, oppressor.[23]

Right-wing media immediately and cynically used Israel's war on Gaza to direct what is essentially wartime propaganda against universities, as well as their professors, administrators, and students. They set out the strategy of placing universities as allies of Hamas *from the very beginning*, directly after Hamas's terrorist attack on Israel, and far in advance of student protests against Israel's response. The propaganda prepared its audience to view the inevitable campus anti-war protests as supporting Hamas—no matter what their form or content. This has proven an effective method of intimidating universities. India has met student protests against anti-Muslim laws with harsh police crackdowns, decrying universities as traitorous to the nation.[24] More generally, American fascist politicians target American universities by describing them as anti-American, just as Russia's fascist politicians attack Russia's universities by calling them anti-Russian, India's fascist politicians target Indian universities by calling them anti-Indian, and Hungary's fascist politicians attack Hungarian universities by calling them anti-Hungarian.

The shape of the attack on K-12 education is similar for these fascist movements. In India, for example, under Prime Minister Narendra Modi's right-wing leadership, the National Council of Educational Research and Training (NCERT) has modified its widely used textbooks to minimize the importance of the Mughal Empire period of India's history, when Muslims ruled the land in which they are now a minority.[25] This feeds the central myth of Hindu nationalism, that India's true glorious past was religiously pure, and exclusively Hindu. Such erasures of history serve to reinforce the impression that Hindus are an exceptional and uniquely worthy class in India, while Muslims are foreign and undeserving.

In Turkey, the authoritarian leader Recep Tayyip Erdoğan has also overseen drastic changes in that nation's textbooks, and has simultaneously presided over a profound shift in Turkish national identity from a proudly secular society to one in which religion plays a dominant role in public life.

Turkey under Erdoğan has removed references to evolution from its high school curriculum. The new textbooks drastically minimize the history of secularism in the Turkish Republic, suggesting it was inconsequential to the nation's history and replacing it with a national and religious consciousness essentially from the Ottoman era.[26]

As all of these examples show—from the United States and Hungary to India and Turkey—an education system is the foundation upon which a political culture is built. Authoritarians have long understood that when they wish to change the political culture, they must begin by seizing control of education.

In the face of such distortions and erasures of history, the truth seems at a distinct disadvantage. How can ordinary people fight back against these erasures of non-dominant perspectives? To answer this question, we might begin by seeking to understand what fascists fear most about education. Virtually every advancement that society has made toward greater equality began with educators. Black teachers in the Jim Crow era were a bulwark against segregationist propaganda, training the leaders of the Civil Rights Movement and giving Black citizens the tools, in the words of the Harvard historian Jarvis Givens, "to imagine a world outside of the confines of Jim Crow."[27] This is why fascists attack teachers. Democratic education enhances human flourishing, supports human dignity, and shapes children into critical, thoughtful, generous, empathetic citizens. An education that valorizes a national, ethnic, or religious identity, on the other hand, is incapable of doing any of these things, and inconsistent with democracy and human flourishing.

2

Colonizing the Mind

Education for colonial people must inevitably mean unrest and revolt; education, therefore, had to be limited and used to inculcate obedience and servility lest the whole colonial system be overthrown.
—W. E. B. Du Bois, "The White Masters of the World"[1]

The night of the sword and the bullet was followed by the chalk and the blackboard. The physical violence of the battlefield was followed by the psychological violence of the classroom.
—Ngũgĩ wa Thiong'o, *Decolonizing the Mind*[2]

When one group erases the history of another, the latter becomes significantly more vulnerable to domination and conquest. One of the clearest examples of this is the practice of modern colonialism. It is much easier for a colonial power to justify taking land when that land can be represented as lacking a history. When a group of people is represented as having no history, they are being denied any valid claim to the present. Colonialism is an ideal case, perhaps the clearest, for understanding how and why the erasure of history is central to the exercise of power and domination.

Western colonialism relies on a set of presumptions about the nature of history itself. These include the assumption that until a civilization reaches a certain level of sophistication, say with the emergence of writing or discernible hierarchy, it can have no history. When Western colonial powers have invaded indigenous peoples' territories—as in North America, for example—they have ignored their songs and stories infused with the past, their complicated land access systems, their social and political structures, their spiritual traditions and kinship rites, all of which are just as intricately human as Europe's cultural and social practices.

Colonialism consists of myths and representations that center the perspective of the colonizing group, erase the colonized subjects' history, and cast the colonized land as empty or, at the very least, unused. Colonizers justify their project by emphasizing its ostensible civilizing mission, which they claim stands to deliver benefits for the colonized in exchange for their land and resources. These benefits, of course, almost always turn out to be intangible, or less valuable than promised, and serve primarily as a supposed reminder of the colonizer's superiority—things like religion, culture, and, in some cases, narrow vocational training.

British colonialism in Africa is a quintessential example of how this system of hierarchy's myths and representations has been used to justify domination and violence. During the first half of the twentieth century, Britain seized massive quantities of the best agricultural land in Kenya from its largest ethnic group, the Kikuyu. When the Kikuyu temporarily retreated from the land, the colonizers declared it empty and unused, which was all the justification they needed to force the Kikuyu, en masse, into reservations on infertile, dusty lands. The British demanded payment from the Kikuyu even to occupy this land, and required that they provide identification documents to leave, in order to prove that they were going to work on one of the huge properties that were handed out to British settlers. In exchange for the plundered land and resources, Britain provided the Kikuyu with missionary schools, rudimentary medical care, and other services—for which they had to pay fees.

By 1952, the Kikuyu could no longer tolerate the situation, and, together with members of other tribes, such as the Embu and Meru, revolted against British colonial rule, launching what would become known as the Mau Mau rebellion. The rebellion would last until 1960, waged by a fighting force they called the Land and Freedom Army, and was violently suppressed, under a so-called Emergency.

In her Pulitzer Prize–winning book, *Imperial Reckoning: The Untold Story of Britain's Gulag in Kenya*, the historian Caroline Elkins details the horrors that British colonial officials perpetrated against suspected Mau Mau rebels and civilians alike. Holding Kikuyu prisoners in concentration camps, the British tortured them for days, supposedly to extract information, but also to force them to confess their Mau Mau sympathies, in a process called screening. Countless Kikuyu died as a result of this widespread and official practice, though we will never know exactly how many, since the British destroyed their records of the camps. During the Emergency, the British were aided and abetted by loyalist collaborators among the Kikuyu, many of whom had attended British schools or found ways to personally profit from the colonizer's seizure of their people's land.[3]

Because Kikuyu customs, traditions, and society were so different from British assumptions about them, the damage inflicted on this group was even more wide-ranging and fundamentally destabilizing than the damage was for tribes that had traditions and customs closer to British expectations. The British system of colonial indirect rule, as Caroline Elkins writes, was:

> . . . a way of administering the empire on the cheap by co-opting local African leaders, using them to enforce discipline and control over local populations, and in return providing them with generous material rewards. Such a system was predicated on the European stereotype of traditional African political systems, which always placed the chief at the top of the hierarchy; the chief, in turn, had the fundamental role of maintaining "tribal order."

But the Kikuyu did not have chiefs. Prior to colonialism, they were a stateless society, governed by
councils of elders and lineage heads. In Kikuyu dis-
tricts these new chiefs were a phenomenon of colonial
rule. They were created by the colonial government
and thus wholly illegitimate in the eyes of ordinary
Kikuyu people.[4]

The chiefs appointed by the British ended up illegiti-
mately seizing the best of the Kikuyu land, and exploiting the
Kikuyu in ways that were almost as extreme as what the British themselves did. Kikuyu British loyalists used their elevated status to exploit other Kikuyu for profit and gain. For
this, they were handsomely rewarded by the British with massive tracts of desirable Kikuyu land.

British colonialism not only dismantled the traditional
governing structures of Kikuyu society but also aimed to
completely eliminate the traditional Kikuyu religion, as well.
This religion, like Judaism, is constituted in large part by
practices, and not mainly by beliefs. These practices were
deeply interwoven into the fabric of Kikuyu society, and in
the rituals and ceremonies of which it is composed, such as
the planting ceremony, whose purpose is to pray for good
crops. The British deliberately structured their institutions
with the aim of annihilating this religion.

Kenyan philosopher Ngũgĩ wa Thiong'o's book *Decolonizing the Mind* describes the effects of colonialism on many

of the colonized—and, in particular, how the colonial system of education led some Kikuyu (and other colonized people) to identify with the colonizers. Thiong'o calls this process "the cultural bomb":

> The effect of a cultural bomb is to annihilate a people's belief in their names, in their languages, in their environment, in their heritage of struggle, in their unity, in their capacities and ultimately in themselves. It makes them see their past as one wasteland of non-achievement and it makes them want to distance themselves from that wasteland. It makes them want to identify with that which is furthest removed from themselves; for instance, with other peoples' languages rather than their own. It makes them identify with that which is decadent and reactionary, all those forces which would stop their own springs of life. It even plants serious doubts about the moral rightness of struggle.[5]

Alliance High School is Kenya's premier boarding school, and counts among its graduates some of Kenya's most powerful politicians and leaders over the decades, including the former attorney general Charles Njonjo, the politician Jaramogi Oginga Odinga (who was also the father of Prime Minister Raila Odinga), and Philip Ndegwa, who served as governor of the Central Bank of Kenya, chairman of the National Bank of Kenya, and chairman of Kenya Airways. Founded by Christian missionaries in 1926, the school prides itself to this day on its religious identity; for example, grace is said before every meal. Thiong'o himself attended Alliance in the 1950s, and recounts some of his experiences there in another of his books:

> At Alliance, the word *truth* was always in the air. But there, it was more like a preexisting entity; all we had to do was accept it. In fact, all we had to do to possess it was to kneel before the Cross. No, not possess it but let it possess us, a civilized spirit possession. One Truth for all. Unchanging. Eternal. It was a faith-dependent Truth.[6]

As Thiong'o sees it, the British educational institutions in Kenya—and throughout East Africa, for that matter—served to perpetuate the same logic of colonialism that had its roots in the so-called Scramble for Africa and the 1884 Berlin conference in which it culminated, where the European powers arbitrarily divided the continent's territories among themselves. Most importantly, for Thiong'o, was the erasure of traditional African languages and their replacement by European ones. Language, he writes, "was the most important vehicle through which that power fascinated and held the soul prisoner. The bullet was the means of the physical subjugation. Language was the means of the spiritual subjugation."[7]

The cultural destruction followed directly from the physical genocide during the Mau Mau rebellion. As it happens, my father, Manfred Stanley, studied this exact topic as a PhD student in Anthropology. He wrote his dissertation, *Heritage of Change: British Education and the Making of an African Intelligentsia*, while living in Kenya just before independence, in the years 1959–62. The dissertation is a study of the first generation of Western-educated Kikuyu, and looks specifically at students whose entire education took place in British schools in Kenya and Uganda. In it, he lays bare how the British education system carried out a form of cultural erasure, which we now recognize as genocidal. My father's field notes reveal that at least part of his interest in this history stemmed from his own childhood in Berlin under National Socialism. As he saw it, there was a straight line between colonialism and fascism, and his desire to understand this connection is what drove much of his research. He did not see himself as analogous to the Kenyans and Ugandans he studied—but he did see how the Nazi fascists and the British colonialists shared certain sensibilities and impulses.

He was certainly not the first scholar to make the comparison, and his work built on that of many other writers and theorists who came before him in the post-colonial tradition. Perhaps most memorably, the Martinican poet, essayist, and politician Aimé Césaire formulated the connection in his classic work *Discourse on Colonialism*, first published in French in 1950. Europeans, he wrote, "tolerated . . . Nazism before it was inflicted on them . . . they absolved it, shut their eyes to it, legitimized it, because, until then, it had been applied only to non-European peoples."[8] Hannah Arendt, in her 1951 book *The Origins of Totalitarianism*, clearly emphasized the linkages between European fascism and the Scramble for Africa.

More recently, the historian Timothy Snyder has argued that Germany's loss of its African colonies in the Treaty of Versailles, at the end of World War I, was part of what led Hitler to turn his attention eastward.[9] The Nazi education system clearly emphasized the narrative that Germany had been wronged. And according to Lisa Pine, another historian of Nazi Germany, colonial geography was one of the "key topics" of the regime's education program, which inculcated in students a belief in "the need to reclaim Germany's lost colonies" and "the history of Germany's colonial achievements."[10]

The education that African students received in the British colonial education system was a British education in every way. Of all the subjects they covered, the schools devoted the greatest amount of time and attention to the Christian Bible. Students also studied the history of European monarchies, learned the names of Britain's kings and queens, and read the classics of English literature. They learned nothing of their own history or religious practices—and indeed, for a time, the British considered anyone practicing the traditional Kikuyu religion to be a potential rebel. The Mau Mau resistance, students were taught, was not political, but "psychopathological."[11] The curriculum, ultimately, was designed to lead students inexorably to the conclusion that the British Empire's actions were justifiable and sound.

In my father's field notes, he writes of the profound racism underlying the British response to the rebellion. He mentions specifically an official report from a British official named F. D. Corfield, titled *The Origins and Growth of Mau Mau*. After meeting with the Kikuyu families of several students he was working with, my father wrote about this report:

> . . . typical for the Corfield Report [was] a deep blindness to sociological, economic and policy reasons for Mau Mau and a tendency to substitute concepts like primitive reversion of savagery, psycho-analytic patterns, etc. It was obvious that Corfield had not—or didn't show any sign of having sat with people like these and actually traced the course of Mau Mau through specific villages' families and personalities.[12]

The British education system in Kenya, my father repeatedly emphasizes in his notes, rested on an assumption that African students are irredeemably "other." As someone who believed that treating others with dignity and respect should be a baseline for all human interaction, he found this unconscionable. Colonialism, like the Nazism he encountered as a child, not only condoned but also required the violation of that baseline.

The British, obviously, were not the only colonial power to wield its cultural might against an indigenous population. The historian David Wallace Adams, in his classic book on American Indian boarding schools in the late nineteenth and early twentieth centuries, discusses how colonialism operated in the subjugation of the indigenous peoples of the United States. These schools relied on what Adams calls "the civilization savagism paradigm," a belief in the importance of education and religion as vehicles by which colonizers bring civilization to the colonized, in order to free them from their "savagism." As Adams writes, "Policymakers had always regarded the Indians' conversion to Christianity as essential." The schools encouraged students to see Christianity as the core of civilization. The superintendent of one school, according to Adams, summarized the urgency of his duty this way: ". . . a really civilized people cannot be found in the world except where the Bible has been sent and the gospel taught; hence we believe that the Indians must have, as an essential part of their education, Christian training."[13]

Much of Ngugi wa Thiong'o's work is devoted to explaining how the British cultivated their Kikuyu loyalist collaborators. And in Adams's account of the American Indian boarding schools, we can see some of the same dynamics at play. At least some of the students in those schools ended up accepting (or, in any case, claiming to accept) the ideology they were taught. Adams quotes one indigenous student forcefully arguing for Western superiority: "Christian nations are the greatest—Christian civilization is the greatest. So if we hope to succeed and make our people who are last, among the first, we must carry to them Christian knowledge, Christian example, and Christian civilization."[14]

According to the ideology of North America's European colonizers, their genocide of the indigenous population, surely one of the worst in history, was justified as a means of bringing civilization to people they understood as "savages." One 1852 textbook offers a typical European view of indigenous people, stating that they "delight in war" and that prior to the arrival of the colonizers they had "worshipped a Good Spirit, and an evil Spirit. But of the true God they knew nothing; nor had they ever heard of the Bible, or of Jesus Christ, the Savior of Men."[15]

The civilization savagism paradigm was driven not only by a perverse sense of religious superiority but also by a view of indigenous people as lazy and in need of responsible guidance in order to harness their productive capacity. According to the same 1852 textbook, indigenous Americans would be capable of ascending "the ladder of civilization" only if they "sever all ties with the past: their communal lifeways, their barbaric religious rituals, and perhaps most important their aversion to manual labor."[16] By the logic of colonialism, white civilization is the only force capable of directing humanity to a productive purpose, which usually happens to be manual labor.

The same dynamic can be found in other places touched by US colonialism. Richard Armstrong was a Christian missionary who founded a handful of schools and churches in Hawai'i and in 1847 was appointed its minister of public instruction by King Kamehameha III. Armstrong brought a colonialist mindset to this position. Writing about Hawaiians, Armstrong stated "this is a lazy people, and if they are ever to be made industrious the work must begin with the young. So I am making strenuous efforts to have some sort of manual labor connected with every school . . . without industry they cannot be moral."

Armstrong's son Samuel Chapman Armstrong would go on to establish the Hampton Normal and Agricultural Institute, a school for Black students in Hampton, Virginia, in 1868. According to the website of Hampton University, the university that eventually grew out of the Hampton Institute, the younger Armstrong's purpose in founding the school was "to train selected Negro youth who should go out and teach and lead their people first by example, by getting land and homes; to give them not a dollar that they could earn for themselves; to teach respect for labor, to replace stupid drudgery with skilled hands, and in this way to build up an industrial system for the sake not only of self-support and intelligent labor, but also for the sake of character."[17] Samuel explicitly linked the mission of the Hampton Institute to the colonialist project that his father had been a part of in Hawaii, writing that the missionary schools his father supervised, "suggested the plan of the Hampton School."[18]

The continuity between American colonialism in territories such as Hawai'i and the country's exploitation of Black Americans at home did not go unnoticed by Black Americans. According to Yale historian Matthew Frye Jacobson:

> Among the most common concerns expressed by black dissenters was that, in this period of Jim Crow legislation, massive disenfranchisement, and rampant antiblack violence and lynching at home, the United States was simply going to export a bitter cargo of Mississippi or Louisiana-style practices abroad. This became a running theme in African American commentary, beginning with the annexation of Hawai'i, which Richmond Planet editor John Mitchell characterized immediately as "The Rape of the Islands."[19]

In both instances, the exploitation of labor was justified as an important element of America's civilizing mission, in keeping with the dehumanizing logic of colonialism, which reduces people to their capacity for manual labor.

Booker T. Washington, who in 1881 established the Tuskegee Institute, was himself a graduate of Hampton, and an ardent admirer of its founder Samuel Chapman Armstrong's educational philosophy, which he knew full well derived from the elder Armstrong's colonialist schools in Hawai'i.[20] The disagreement between Washington and the sociologist and activist W. E. B. Du Bois is one of the most famous American public debates, and neatly represents two starkly different potential responses to colonialist logic. In his public writings, Washington urged Black Americans to prioritize industrial education over political education, and thus to place greater emphasis on their productive potential as workers than on their identity as democratic citizens. As Du Bois saw it, this approach served white supremacy. He counseled Black American citizens instead to seek a liberal education, whose purpose was not only to elevate the soul but also to give them skills to democratically advance their own interests.[21]

In settler colonialism, the process by which colonists seize land and permanently displace its indigenous inhabitants, the very existence of those inhabitants must be concealed or minimized, and the land represented as empty. Consider this passage from a 1983 edition of the widely used textbook *The American Pageant*:[22]

> The American Republic, which is still relatively young when compared with the Old World, was from the outset richly favored. It started from scratch on a vast and virgin continent, which was so sparsely populated by Indians that they could be eliminated or

shouldered aside. Such a magnificent opportunity for a great democratic experiment may never come again, for no other huge, fertile, and relatively uninhabited areas are left in the temperate zones of this crowded planet.[23]

In a section titled "Columbus Stumbles Upon a New World," the authors present Columbus not as a genocidal colonialist bent on exploiting indigenous people for material gain, but as a heroic adventurer. Furthermore, they reinforce the colonialist narrative of an empty land by wildly understating the indigenous population of the Americas (the best scholarly estimates put the number at the time of Columbus's arrival at around 72 million):

> Most native settlements were small, scattered, and often impermanent. So thinly spread across the land was the North American Indian population that large areas were virtually uninhabited, with whispering, primeval forests and sparkling, virgin waters. Perhaps one million Indians dwelled in all of the present-day United States at the time of Columbus' discovery....[24]

This narrative of an empty land has also been used to legitimize colonialist practices in the Middle East. Complicating the claim that Israel is a settler colonial nation is that the largest ethnic group of Jewish people in Israel are Mizrahi, most of whom are indigenous to the region. But the *European* Jewish people, the Ashkenazi, who originally came to

Palestine *did* regard it as a colonial project. The majority of Ashkenazi Jews who came to Palestine in the nineteenth century spoke of their experience as one of entering an empty land with no civilized settlements. David Ben-Gurion, the first prime minister of Israel, wrote in a 1952 essay that after Israel's war of independence, known to Palestinians as the *Nakba* (the "catastrophe" in Arabic), which "brought ruin and destruction on hundreds of settlements . . . there stood only the Jewish villages established in the last 70 years and a few which were not Jewish. The truth is that the state inherited a wasted and deserted land."[25]

According to the Israeli researcher Noga Kadman's 2015 book, *Erased from Space and Consciousness: Israel and the Depopulated Palestinian Villages of 1948*, in Israel's self-understanding its founding was part of "a process of redemption of 'uninhabited' and 'empty land' from historical oblivion and from a social and geographical void."[26] To promote this myth, Israeli forces drove many of the land's inhabitants out, then destroyed and removed their villages, which numbered well over four hundred according to some estimates.[27] Over the next few decades, the Israeli government has obviously engaged colonialist practices directed against lands still occupied by Palestinians. This process, which Kadman calls Judaization of the space, made it seem that Jewish populations simply moved into previously unused and empty land. More generally, the slogan that one of the central Jewish accomplishments was "making the desert bloom" is an example of a straightforwardly colonialist mindset, on equal standing with the claim that Europeans brought civilization to the Americas. The slogan only makes sense if one dehumanizes the previous occupants of the land, or simply erases their presence.[28]

During the war in Gaza kicked off by the Hamas terrorist attack on Israel in October 2023 and the seizure of more than two hundred hostages, Israel mercilessly bombed civilian targets in Gaza, claiming that Hamas was using these sites as a cover for its operations. Among these targets were Gazan universities, schools, and museums. As the *Toronto Star* columnist Shree Paradkar explained at the time, this specific type of destruction constitutes what some observers call scholasticide. This involves "the destruction of Gaza's educational infrastructure, assaults on universities in Gaza and West Bank, as well as serious harassment and attacks on senior faculty and students supporting Palestine within the Israeli university system." As Paradkar points out, scholasticide "risks erasing Gaza's past. . . . With archives and architecture destroyed, it's as if Palestinians never lived there."[29] And on April 18, 2024, over a dozen members of the Special Procedures of the Human Rights Council, including the Special Rapporteur on the right to education, Farida Shaheed, put out a statement expressing profound concern about scholasticide in Gaza.[30]

Israel's continuing erasure of the Palestinian past, and

even the *recent* Palestinian past, gives many people in Israel and elsewhere the pretext to reject legitimate Palestinian claims to the land of their ancestors, as well as any reparations for this loss. And it denies Palestinians the claim to peoplehood, rendering them stateless—which, as Hannah Arendt emphasized in her work on fascism, is an extraordinarily precarious position.[31]

The ideology of colonialism takes the form, in schools and public culture, of erasing vital history, representing the colonized group as being without history. Colonial education not only erases history; it also misrepresents it, suggesting that the colonized population is savage, lazy, and corrupt. White Christian Nationalism is responsible for brutal practices of colonization in Africa and the Americas. Israel's colonialist practices are also a result of identity-based nationalism, in this case, Jewish nationalism. We have explored here how various identity-based nationalisms are used to justify violent colonialist practices. It is time now to turn to nationalism on its own, and as an educational practice.

3

The Nationalist Project

> It is one of the strange throughlines in the history of
> U.S. nationalism that since at least the mid-nineteenth
> century, Americans have fancied their country as the
> savior of the world's peoples—redeemer nation, civ-
> ilizer, beacon of liberty, asylum of the oppressed—
> even as they have expressed profound anxiety that the
> world's people might ultimately prove the ruin of the
> republic.
>
> —Matthew Frye Jacobson, *Barbarian Virtues*[1]

I n his early-nineteenth-century work *Addresses to the German Nation*, the German philosopher Johann Gottlieb
Fichte makes a case for what he sees as the objective greatness
of his homeland. This greatness, Fichte claims, is evident in
the grandeur of the German language, and in certain simi-
larities that he traces between Germany and Ancient Greece.
"The Germans still speak a living language," he writes, "and
have done so ever since it first streamed forth from nature,
whereas the other Teutonic tribes speak a language that stirs
only on the surface but is dead at the root."[2] One of the book's
main goals is to formulate a new model of national public

education aimed at instilling "the higher love of fatherland." However, Fichte's idea that the German language is somehow more "living" than other languages has not survived centuries of science. His argument for an elemental similarity between the German nation and Ancient Greece also collapses under any measure of scrutiny.

In Fichte's time, the Habsburg Empire officially recognized fourteen languages, including German, Hungarian, Italian, Polish, and Romanian. National identities arose based in large part on these languages, threatening the empire. The twentieth-century scholar Benedict Anderson, who published pioneering work arguing that all nations are essentially alike in how they arise and establish their cultures, also studied this early form of nationalism based on shared languages, which he traced to the increasing prevalence at the time of print technologies such as books and newspapers. "The convergence of capitalism and print technology," he writes, "created the possibility of a new form of imagined community, which in its basic morphology set the stage for the modern nation."[3] Based on this understanding, theorists of nationalism who see national identity as stemming from language often link languages to other features, such as culture, history, and traditions.

The type of nationalism that undergirds colonialism involves a self-aggrandizing conception of the nation, one that justifies its dominion over others. I will call this *supremacist nationalism.* Supremacist nationalism can take either a universalist or a non-universalist form. According to the universalist form, which relies on the "civilization savagism paradigm" discussed in the previous chapter, the colonizing nation is justified in its domination of others because of its status as the standard-bearer of civilization. According to the non-universalist form, the colonizing nation is justified simply because of its military power. The line between these two versions is thin. The "civilization savagism paradigm" on which the former rests is, of course, fictitious. And *in practice* at least, both versions can be similar in their brutality.

Nationalism can also be *anti-colonial*—as in the case of the nationalism that motivated the Mau Mau rebellion in Kenya, for example—and anti-colonial nationalism, too, comes in both universal and non-universal forms. According to the former, each nation has its own traditions but shares in a common universal humanity that places obligations of equal respect and dignity for other cultures. This is a familiar kind of Enlightenment liberalism, albeit one that sees common humanity and the duties for equal respect to all fellow humans. The latter kind of anti-colonial nationalism emerged during the Enlightenment, rejecting the era's ideals and using the opposition as a basis for resisting the colonial enterprises those ideals were used, usually cynically, to support.

The twentieth-century philosopher Isaiah Berlin devoted considerable time and energy to studying and describing this "counter-Enlightenment," which rejected notions of progress and universal reason. One proponent of the movement whom Berlin studied in particular was the eighteenth-century philosopher Johann Gottfried von Herder, who had argued that different cultures are incommensurable, and that there is no universal standard of civilizational progress. Part of what attracted Berlin to Herder was that he rejected his Enlightenment opponents' justifications for race-based colonialism and slavery, which they saw as working in service of a civilizing mission. As Berlin writes,

> colonial subjugation of native populations, ancient and modern, in and outside Europe, is always represented [in Herder's work] as being morally odious and a crime against humanity.... The shamans of central Asia, he insists, are not just deceivers; nor are myths simply false statements invented by wicked priests to bamboozle and acquire power over the masses . . . to foist a set of alien values on another Nation (as missionaries have done in the Baltic providences, and are doing, for example, in India) is both ineffective and harmful.[4]

Herder was, as Berlin had it, "one of the leaders of the romantic revolt against classicism, rationalism, and faith in the scientific method."[5] Herder's philosophy, based on the incomparability of cultures and the untranslatability of languages, provided a powerful foundation for these anti-Enlightenment positions.

While it may be tempting to assume that Enlightenment ideals such as universal moral personhood draw a clear line of distinction between supremacist and anti-colonial nationalisms, this is not the case. Enlightenment ideals can be used to support both kinds of nationalism. Universalism can be used to fight colonialism, by appeal to the common humanity of (for example) indigenous groups facing colonization. Universalism has also been regularly *misused* in the colonialist project, to exclude populations from equal respect—for example, by deeming some populations "savage" and hence outside the boundaries of universal moral personhood.

In the United States' earliest days, a brutal form of supremacist nationalism arose as a way of justifying some of the country's deepest sins, including chattel slavery and indigenous dispossession. It has survived in part through accounts of the country's history that glorify the deeds of white Europeans while erasing the contributions of Black and indigenous Americans. The Yale historian Ned Blackhawk's 2023 book, *The Rediscovery of America: Native Peoples and the Unmaking of U.S. History*, is an attempt to reckon with this myth. Blackhawk writes, "American historians have long assumed the nation's history to be that of Europeans and white Americans. Histories of early American religion, economy, and political ideology have, accordingly, fallen into separate fields of inquiry that often examine only the experiences of settlers."[6]

In parts of the United States where this narrative holds especially strong influence, politicians such as Texas governor Greg Abbott have aggressively fought back against academic efforts to cover the full story of the country's history. A number of these politicians have begun to take their cues on educational matters not from academics, or even the well-funded think tanks often responsible for reductive, anti-intellectual curricula, but from entertainers. One example is the right-wing talk show host Dennis Prager, whose political-messaging group PragerU has in recent years become an approved educational resource provider in Oklahoma, Florida, New Hampshire, Montana, and Arizona. Despite its misleading name, PragerU is not in any sense an academic institution. The organization is more connected with right-wing talk radio than anything else, and is broadly devoted to spreading far-right narratives by creating and disseminating videos online directed at school-age children.

In a video characteristic of its offerings, *Christopher Columbus: Explorer of the New World*, a boy makes the case for Christopher Columbus as an important heroic figure. Columbus, the boy explains, "was a really courageous guy who loved exploring, inspired generations, and spread Christianity and Western civilization to people who really benefited from new ways of thinking and doing things." The girl with whom he is speaking responds, "That sounds really good!" In the rest of the video, the boy and the girl travel back in time to meet a friendly Columbus, who tells his life story and decries the practice of measuring his actions against future standards of behavior.[7]

In fact, the scale and enormity of what we would now call the genocidal actions of Spanish conquistadors were clearly recognized at the time. In 1542, Bartolomé de las Casas wrote a book titled *A Short Account of the Destruction of the Indies*, in which he described and denounced the multiple genocides of indigenous people in the West Indies he witnessed in the decades after Columbus's arrival. "The Spaniards have shown not the slightest consideration for these people," he writes. "They have had as little concern for their souls as for their bodies, all the millions that perished having gone to their deaths with no knowledge of God and without the benefit of the sacraments." The book contains almost unreadable descriptions of the horrors that the conquistadors perpetrated on the indigenous people of the West Indies, including roasting people alive on spits and tearing pregnant women apart, among many others.[8] Any narrative that presents the European arrival in the Americas as part of a glorious "age of exploration," and not an age of multiple genocides, suppresses the perspectives of both indigenous Americans and Europeans such as Bartolomé de las Casas who unambiguously recognized the unspeakable brutality being committed.

Supremacist nationalism does not recognize the nation's past sins, or at best drastically minimizes them. In the case of the United States, this means the erasure of the perspectives of both indigenous people subjected to genocide, and Black Americans who experienced slavery and Jim Crow. Dubious online content generators like PragerU continue a past narrative of erasures. Consider the work of the Virginia History and Textbook Commission, which was formed in 1950 to design educational resources for the state with the goal of defending the white supremacist perspective. One of the textbooks it produced, titled *Virginia: History, Government, Geography*, contained staggering misrepresentations of history. The 1957 edition, for instance, had this to say about slavery:

> Many slave masters did not like to have the state government meddle in what they considered their private business. They managed their servants according to their own methods. They knew the best way to control their slaves was to win their confidence and affection.
>
> Many Negroes were taught to read and write. Many of them were allowed to meet in groups for preaching, for funerals, and for singing and dancing. They went visiting at night and sometimes owned guns and other weapons. . . .
>
> Life among the Negroes of Virginia in slavery times was generally happy. The Negroes went about in a cheerful manner making a living for themselves and for those for whom they worked. They were not so unhappy as some Northerners thought they were, nor were they so happy as some Southerners claimed. The Negroes had their problems and their troubles.

But they were not worried by the furious arguments going on between Northerners and Southerners over what should be done with them. In fact, they paid little attention to these arguments.[9]

The Virginia textbook, of course, was part of a larger effort to discount the atrocities of slavery in the United States by representing enslaved Black Americans as content with their situation, and uninterested in the struggle for their own liberation.

One PragerU video called "A Short History of Slavery" demonstrates the ease with which one can superficially integrate the subject of slavery into a curriculum, while erasing any real account of its significance or its harms. The video is narrated by the Black far-right commentator Candace Owens, and takes pains to omit the contributions of Black people in fighting for their freedom, crediting white men for having rescued the world from slavery. According to Owens:

> White people were the first to formally put an end to slavery. In 1833, Britain was the first country in the history of the world to pass a slavery abolition act. They were quickly followed by France, who in 1848 abolished slavery in her many colonies. Then, of course, came the Thirteenth Amendment in the United States Constitution. After centuries of human slavery, white men led the world in putting an end to the abhorrent practice. That includes the three hundred thousand Union soldiers, overwhelmingly white, who died during the Civil War.[10]

Owens neglects to mention Haiti, the first country in history to be born from a successful slave rebellion, which began in 1791. She seems ignorant of the fact that Haiti, not Britain, was the first country to abolish slavery, in 1793. And Owens omits entirely the significant role that Black Americans played in their own liberation during the Civil War.

The video also, bizarrely, seems to downplay the harms of slavery itself, repeating the arguments of European colonial powers that defended their violent plundering of Africa by claiming that they had protected Africans from being exploited by one another. Belgium, for instance, justified its brutal colonization of the Congo under King Leopold II by the claim that it had also saved Africans from being enslaved by other Africans and sold to Arab slave traders. But in fact, it was no salvation at all. Under directives from King Leopold II, perhaps as many as 10 million Africans in the Congo were murdered as part of a brutal effort to force them to harvest rubber—amounting to one of the worst crimes in human history. Owens's PragerU video, however, uncritically accepts the narrative of the Belgian colonists:

> The truth is that Africans were sold into slavery *by other Black Africans.* And in many cases sold for items as trivial as gin and mirrors. Whites didn't go into the interior and round up the natives. They waited on the coast for their Black partners to bring them Black bodies. The stark reality is that our lives had *very little value* to our ancestors.[11]

This narrative not only excuses the atrocities committed by Europeans in Africa but also serves to downplay any hardships faced by the descendants of enslaved peoples. By Owens's reasoning, it could even be argued that whatever harms or systemic obstacles that Black people in the United States have dealt with over the centuries were preferable to the conditions they would have faced had their ancestors remained in Africa.

The United States' Reconstruction era, the brief period directly following the United States' Civil War, when the federal government saw to it that formerly enslaved Black Americans were allowed to participate in the civic life for the first time, came to a violent end in under a decade. Between 1865 and 1877, sixteen Black Americans took office as elected congressmen and many hundreds served in state legislatures and as local officials. As the era came to an end, the forces opposed to granting Black people full citizenship, which had been temporarily defeated by the Civil War, quickly began formulating an alternative version of events intended to cast the period as a failed experiment, and to justify revoking the limited rights and privileges the South's Black population had briefly enjoyed.

Academic histories of the time, including school textbooks, blamed Black Americans themselves for their loss of these rights and privileges. In a textbook from the 1930s, *American History*, the Reconstruction period is described as a time marred by Black political corruption and mismanagement:

> The South had not recovered from the war, and the people were in no position to pay heavy taxes. But the negro legislators never thought of that, and they recklessly voted people's money away. The debts of the Southern states increased by leaps and bounds, and the Southern whites were powerless under the law to stop the mad career of the men in office.[12]

The textbook also represents the Ku Klux Klan (KKK) as heroes who rescued the South from this kind of corruption by preventing Black people from voting:

> The South was threatened with ruin unless something was done to break the Negro control. To do this many White men joined secret societies. These societies worked to frighten the Negro into staying away from the polls and to make him realize that the White man was still to run the South. Bands of men in white robes and with fiery crosses rode the highways at night. The superstitious Negroes feared the visits of ghostly night riders who knocked at the cabin door at midnight and in a solemn voice threatened the trembling Negro with terrible punishments. The work of the secret societies had the desired results.[13]

In racist stereotypes dating back to the nineteenth century, US textbooks taught that Black people are naturally inclined toward corruption and mismanagement, and thus not suited for participation in democratic life. When President Donald Trump discounts as illegitimate votes cast in American cities with large Black populations, such as Atlanta, Philadelphia, and Detroit, on the grounds of "corruption," he is evoking this same racist stereotype. The long shadow of historical disinformation stretches over decades, and the myths of the past weigh heavily on the present.

✦　✦　✦

While supremacist nationalisms have flourished all around the world, the United States is home to an especially potent strain known as *American exceptionalism*, which represents the country's founding as innocent, and its westward expansion as justified. To support these claims, the historical narrative of American exceptionalism erases both the central role that slavery played in shaping the country's economy and the vast genocide of indigenous peoples. Ned Blackhawk writes, in many Americans' understanding "the settlement of North America was bloodless. . . . Indians did not constitute foreign states. Nor did they govern their territories. They were either not fully human or lived in primitive forms of development that required uplift."[14]

A central form of American exceptionalism, historically and today, is a version of supremacist nationalism based on race. But even this form is also linked to religion. According to it, America's greatness stems from both its whiteness and its Christianity. By contrast, Aryan nationalism, the form at the heart of German fascism, was a purely racial nationalism and was not grounded in an appeal to religiosity. The biological *race* of Germans, and race alone, was allegedly the source of (supposed) German supremacy.

The common thread between American and German racial nationalism, then, is an ideology of racial supremacy. In both places, this ideology has been employed to justify mass violence against supposed racial "others." As Hannah Arendt explained in her book *The Origins of Totalitarianism*, many twentieth-century genocides were motivated by ideologies of Darwinian racial supremacy, in which "aristocracy was held to be the natural outcome, not of politics, but of natural selection, of pure breeding."[15] According to this ideology, humankind's races are biologically distinct and the supposed cognitive and emotional differences between them account for any sharply different outcomes that we see today—as opposed to, say, the depredations of colonialism, or the effects of structural racism. By this logic, victims of neglect and discrimination are responsible for their own struggles.

It would be easy to conclude from these examples that the myth of biological race is the primary motivation behind supremacist nationalism. There are, however, plenty of historical and contemporary examples in which the ideology is powered by other factors.

A number of violent supremacist nationalist movements are based on religion. The Rashtriya Swayamsevak Sangh (RSS), in India, is a paramilitary organization. Its close cousin, which can be thought of in a sense as its political wing, is the Bharatiya Janata Party (BJP), the country's governing party, which is led by Prime Minister Narendra Modi. Although India was founded as a secular state, the RSS seeks to transform it into an explicitly Hindu state, and works toward this goal by persecuting non-Hindu citizens—primarily the country's large Muslim population, but also Christians and other religious minorities.

Since taking power in May 2014, following the election of Prime Minister Modi, Hindu supremacists have transformed the public sphere—and have placed particular emphasis on establishing their ideology within the country's education system. By August of 2014, just months after coming to power, the RSS had created the Bharatiya Shiksha Niti Ayog, a committee whose purpose was to pressure the education ministry into supporting its Hindu nationalist vision for the country.[16] The National Council of Educational Research and Training (NCERT), meanwhile, has drastically rewritten the textbooks used in public schools throughout India, making over one thousand changes across 182 textbooks, all in support of Hindu nationalism.[17]

The account of Mahatma Gandhi's assassination in history textbooks is a case in point. Gandhi is generally regarded in India as a founding figure and national hero. Yet Hindu supremacists regarded Gandhi's calls for the equitable treatment of Muslims and for peace with the neighboring Muslim nation of Pakistan as traitorous. Indeed, the Hindu supremacist who assassinated Gandhi, Nathuram Vinayak Godse, did so on the grounds that he had been acting in the interests of Muslims. Prior to the RSS's pressure campaign, one textbook produced by the NCERT had emphasized the dangers of Hindu nationalist extremism, clearly labeling Godse as an adherent of this ideology, and explaining how it was a threat to India's emerging secular identity as a home for both Hindus and Muslims. In a version of the same textbook published after BJP's rise to power, however, the section on Gandhi's assassination has been subtly rewritten so as to normalize the Hindu nationalist ideology and absolve its most infamous crime.[18]

According to the tenets of Hindu supremacy, Gandhi's efforts to establish equality between Hindus and Muslims were by their nature anti-Hindu. Gandhi, rather than being the nation's founder, was a traitor. Whereas the pre-Modi textbook explained that Gandhi was motivated primarily by his pursuit of "Hindu-Muslim unity," the revised version describes him as driven by dissatisfaction with "the Indian government's decision not to honour its financial commitments to Pakistan." Gandhi's goal, the textbook implicitly suggests, was to funnel money to Pakistan—a nefarious scheme that cannot be separated, it implies, from his aspiration to extend equal rights to Muslims.

Hindu supremacy represents India as a nation whose Hindu identity stretches back thousands of years and defines the country. It represents both Islam and Christianity as foreign religions associated with the violent colonization and domination of India. It represents secularism, which in fact is fundamental to Indian democracy, as a foreign colonialist intervention. All of this justifies mass violence against non-Hindu populations, who are said to be bringing foreign ideas into India in an effort to destroy the nation's Hindu character.

Hindu supremacist violence in India has been directed against both Christians and Muslims, but Muslims are taken as the primary target. The Hindu supremacists' aim has long been to push Muslims into a state of semi-citizenship, if not rid the nation of them altogether. Even liberals and intellectuals who have simply promoted Indian secularism have suffered terrible fates.

Another movement of nationalist supremacy rooted in religion can be found in Israel, intensifying especially under the far-right government of Prime Minister Benjamin Netanyahu. In July 2018, Israel's legislature, the Knesset, passed a "nation-state law" that formally declared Israel "the Nation-State of the Jewish People" and specified that Jewish people have the sole "right to exercise national self-determination."

The law also codified some long-standing legal practices (for example, governing property) that give Jewish citizens of Israel greater protections than non-Jewish citizens.[19] In doing so, the law makes explicit that the Israeli state is a non-democratic apartheid state—the unsurprising result of a founding ideology premised on erasing the history of the land's previous non-Jewish inhabitants.

The nationalism that motivates Russia's recent genocide in Ukraine is potentially more puzzling conceptually than either Hindu nationalism or Jewish nationalism, since it does not even recognize a difference between Ukrainians and Russians. Russia today is the world's most clearly fascist nation, and the country's 2022 invasion of Ukraine and subsequent operations amount to at least a cultural genocide—involving, for example, the mass removal of Ukrainian children from their families for adoption in Russia. But the form of nationalism that Russia has used to justify its genocidal actions is rooted in neither race, nor religion, nor ethnicity—and for this reason cannot be classified as supremacist. As the Russian nationalists see it, Ukrainians belong to the same race and ethnicity as Russians, and are hiding behind a "fake" Ukrainian identity. Russian president Vladimir Putin spelled this out in a July 2021 speech, in which he declared that Russians and Ukrainians are "one people—a single whole."[20]

In the areas of Ukraine it has occupied since the invasion, Russia has completely suppressed the Ukrainian language, and placed textbooks in the schools that erase any hint of an independent Ukrainian identity. Putin, meanwhile, has reinforced this denial at every turn, and made a habit of referring to the Ukrainian language as "Little Russian," or as a dialect of Russian.[21] Like Johann Gottlieb Fichte, the nineteenth-century German philosopher, Putin sees language as a decisive factor in the determination of national identity—thus, the idea of a Ukrainian language is understood as a grave threat. In one speech denouncing the very concept of "Ukrainian people as a nation separate from the Russians," Putin declared that there was "no historical basis for this" and blamed the notion on "all sorts of concoctions." But as Benedict Anderson points out, the first official Ukrainian grammar appeared in 1819, only seventeen years after the first official Russian grammar. If Ukrainian identity is a "concoction," so too is Russian identity.[22]

Russia also engaged in a similar erasure of Ukrainian autonomy in the period surrounding its 2014 invasion of Eastern Ukraine, which it represented instead as a series of independence movements by self-identified Russian populations in Ukraine. What was in fact an aggressive Russian invasion was represented as legitimate grassroots resistance. A recent Russian textbook, for example, recounts the events this way:

> Portraying the war in Donbas as a civil war without mentioning the Russian presence is a contentious perspective. The deep socio-political crisis that struck

Ukraine in 2013–4 essentially led to the collapse of statehood and the emergence of several separate regions on its territory that were completely beyond the control of the central government.

Resistance in the southern and eastern regions, along with attempts by nationalist "Maidan" activists to seize local administration buildings (February 24 in Kharkiv, February 22–3 in Luhansk), served as a catalyst for the organizational formation of the so-called Resistance movement, initially characterized by regular mass rallies and demonstrations.[23]

Textbooks supposedly covering the "History of Russia" and approved for the eleventh grade by the Russian Ministry of Education in 2022 present a similar narrative.[24] According to one, these areas subsequently chose freely to become part of Russia:

In the autumn-winter of 2013/14, the most acute domestic political crisis erupted in Ukraine. Its most important consequence was the inclusion of two new states, the federation of the Republic of Crimea and Sevastopol both became part of Russia. This happened on the basis of a referendum held in Crimea.[25]

These "history" books do not mention any presence of Russian soldiers involved in Crimea or Donbas, only peaceful transitions to Russian rule, supported by majorities in these territories. Colonial military invasions in the service of violent expansions of empire are here represented as peaceful and voluntary.

The Rwandan genocide is perhaps the clearest example of the horrors to which humans can subject one another without any basis of cultural difference whatsoever. Hutus and Tutsis are two groups in Rwanda that share not only the same language, Kinyarwanda, but also the same traditional religion—surprising commonalities in the most diverse continent in the world (Congo alone has well over two hundred languages). However, the small differences that do exist between these two highly intermarried and integrated groups were accentuated during the Belgian colonization of Rwanda, as the colonialists benefited from dividing the colonized populations. The Hutu Power movement, a virulent form of ethnic nationalism, fomented hatred of Tutsis as a basis of Hutu identity, ultimately planning and carrying out a genocide of Tutsis between April and July of 1994, in which five hundred to eight hundred thousand Tutsis were massacred.[26]

✦ ✦ ✦

The instances of nationalism we have thus far explored have almost invariably fueled—and been fueled by—bigotry and violence. But nationalism is not inevitably bound up in hate. As I have discussed, nationalism can also be anti-colonial. In his classic 1902 work, *Imperialism: A Study*, the English economist J. A. Hobson describes anti-colonial nationalism, emphasizing its compatibility with a cooperative, peaceful ethos of internationalism. As Hobson writes, "the triumph of nationalism seems to have crushed the rising hope of internationalism. Yet it would appear that there is no essential antagonism between them. A true strong internationalism in form or spirit would rather imply the existence of powerful self-respecting nationalities which seek union on the basis of common national needs and interests."[27] Hobson contrasts this anti-colonial nationalism, which is fully consistent with the kind of global cosmopolitan project so often demonized by far-right-wing politicians, with the sort that "glows with the animus of greed and self-aggrandizement."[28]

American exceptionalism, of whatever variety (racial or not), does "glow with the animus of greed and self-aggrandizement." Politicians across the political spectrum in the United States present American exceptionalism as an obvious truth, and it is widely accepted by a majority of the country's citizens. It is used to justify not only America's wars but also its massively disproportionate use of the world's resources, and its disproportionate contributions to climate change.[29] Just as German education in the Weimar period and before embraced an inflated conception of German national identity that paved the way for National Socialism, the widespread devotion to American exceptionalism leaves the United States keenly susceptible to the advances of a disciplined and informed fascist movement of its own, while obscuring this very weakness from its citizens (since American exceptionalism holds that the United States is uniquely resistant to all harmful influences, including fascism).

The same is true in other countries beholden to supremacist nationalism. The contemporary Russian supremacy movement, for instance, holds firm to its belief that Russia is the natural successor to the Soviet empire, and thus should rightfully inherit the neighboring territories that were previously part of the Soviet Union. The Russian state promotes this narrative in every way it can—including through its deft manipulation (and sometimes outright control) of the media, as well as through the textbooks it sanctions, which have consistently erased the worst of the country's crimes, especially those directed against Ukraine.

The most significant of these omissions pertains to Holodomor, a genocide of the Ukrainian people, in which millions of Ukrainian peasants starved to death after Stalin demanded draconian requisitions of grain from them, knowing full well that this would have devastating consequences.[30] In Ukrainian and Russian, the term "Holodomor" consists of two parts: "famine" and "to kill" or "make someone suffer"—the closest translation is essentially "someone making others starve intentionally." Importantly, although the word "Holodomor" and the tragedy it represents are well known throughout both countries, Russian textbooks describe the event using the generic term for "famine," implying that Holodomor was merely a bureaucratic accident, and one that affected all of the USSR equally.[31] In Ukrainian textbooks, it is represented as a famine that Stalin inflicted specifically upon the Ukrainians, which is considerably closer to the truth.

✦ ✦ ✦

While real-world examples may be rare, it is not difficult to imagine the sort of anti-colonial nationalism that J. A. Hobson described—one that is designed not to absolve the nation of its sins, but rather to push it to fulfill its highest ideals. What would anti-colonial nationalism look like in America? It would be a view according to which Americans are bound by an important common interest (for example, in democracy) and engaged in the shared project of elevating living standards for all. One could be proud to be an American because of its natural beauty, its cultural productions, its wondrous cities, and its diverse population without believing that America is the greatest nation in human history. This kind of American nationalism would be anti-colonial, committed to a distinctly American project of nurturing its vast diversity rather than suppressing it, while also addressing structural problems of inequality. By its very nature, this program would acknowledge the country's past sins, yet would also recognize that it still retains great promise. An education system based on anti-colonial American nationalism would, in nearly every way, run counter to the nationalist curricula pushed by far-right American politicians today—which minimize the horrors of slavery, indigenous genocide, and their present-day consequences. Its schools would teach history that highlights rather than obscures the effects of structural racism—a necessary first step toward eliminating it.

We can also recognize a form of anti-colonial nationalism in the post-war West German education system, which strongly connected German identity to liberal democratic forms of life. For example, it granted students a high degree of autonomy, in the form of student government and influence on curricula, encouraging them to resist subordination to fascist forms of authority. It emphasized values such as tolerance, and sought to make them a central part of post-war German identity. And perhaps most importantly, it for the most part addressed Germany's recent past directly and honestly, seeking to connect German social identity to an attempt to atone for the country's past sins, rather than hide from them in shame.

And yet even here, in this self-consciously non-supremacist education system, there were problems. Schools taught, for instance, that Auschwitz was in Poland, and that it was run by a group of particularly terrible Germans, the SS, who directed a largely Slavic population of guards and kapos to undertake the mass killings characteristic of Nazi rule.

As a student in Germany in 1985 and 1986, I found this

bewildering. Some members of my mother's family were shot over pits presumably by ordinary Wehrmacht soldiers, not the SS officers who ran Hitler's death camps. My Polish uncle had spent four years in a small Nazi labor camp, not a death camp. Three times during his incarceration in this camp, he was led out to be executed, each time escaping this fate by happenstance.

Almost every German I met had grandparents who fought on the Eastern Front—these were supposedly the "innocent Germans." But were the soldiers who shot most of my family members really innocent of Germany's crimes? Were those who ran Germany's labor camps innocent of these crimes? It was not until the twenty-first century, when the concept of the *Holocaust by Bullets* was formulated, that historians came to recognize that over a million additional Jews were murdered during World War II outside of Europe's concentration camps, by ordinary Wehrmacht soldiers in the manner of my great-uncles and their children. But the German school I attended did not broach such matters. In so doing, it was falsely minimizing the scale of Germany's crimes, and absolving "the ordinary German" of guilt.[32]

The forms of nationalism involved in anti-colonial struggles, or related freedom struggles, such as Black liberation, are nationalisms of oppressed people and hence not obviously supremacist. But it would be wrong to think that nationalisms of formerly or even currently oppressed people are immune to the worst impulses of supremacist nationalism. In the case of Israel, a group that was in all other countries a national minority became a political majority. This eventually resulted in a widespread supremacist colonial nationalism, which has been directed against Palestinians. In the case of India, the Hindu majority freed themselves from outside colonial domination, only to use their newfound autonomy in service of dominating the country's Muslim minority.

History shows that in a victorious power struggle against a violent colonizer, the new group in power can replicate the colonizer's actions. Ideally, the shift in power should also prompt a shift in attitudes and goals. As the anti-colonial philosopher Frantz Fanon saw it:

> When it is achieved during a war of liberation the mobilization of the masses introduces the notion of common cause, national destiny, and collective history into every consciousness. Consequently, . . . nation building is facilitated by the existence of this mortar kneaded with blood and rage. . . . During the colonial period the people were called upon to fight against oppression. Following national liberation they are urged to fight against poverty, illiteracy, and underdevelopment.[33]

The problem with nation-building projects arising from ethnic or religious nationalism is that often they fail to make this shift. Attention that was once directed to an outside colonial oppressor is shifted not to a productive struggle against poverty or inequality—but to a struggle against political opponents and various chosen scapegoats.

The nineteenth-century sociologist Émile Durkheim could also see a clear distinction between inward- and outward-facing nationalisms, one of which he endorses and the other of which he warns against:

> Everything depends, after all, on the way in which patriotism is conceived; it can take two different forms. Insofar as it is centrifugal, so to speak, it points national activity outside its boundaries and prompts nations to encroach upon one another, to stress their incompatibilities. Then they are put in a situation of conflict and, at the same time, put national sentiment in conflict with commitments to mankind. Or, conversely, the sentiment of patriotism may be altogether internally oriented, fixing upon the tasks of the internal improvement of society. In this case, it prompts all nations that have achieved comparable moral development to collaborate toward the same end. The first way is aggressive, military; the second is scientific, artistic, and, in a word, basically pacific.[34]

These words were from lectures delivered well before the advent of European fascism. But Durkheim's remarks were prescient about the dangers inherent to certain versions of European nationalism.

All nationalisms, including anti-colonial ones, are based on some form of myth, some form of "imagined community," in Benedict Anderson's famous words. The myths of supremacist nationalism have however a specific structure, one that represents the nation as greater than its neighbors, and its national sins ultimately as triumphs. In so doing, supremacist nationalism lays the basis for fascism.

4

From Supremacism to Fascism

Everything we admire on this earth today—science and art, technology and inventions—is only the creative product of a few peoples and originally perhaps of *one* race. On them depends the existence of this whole culture. If they perish, the beauty of this earth will sink into the grave with them.

—Adolf Hitler, *Mein Kampf* [1]

The goal of female education must invariably be the future mother.

—Adolf Hitler, *Mein Kampf* [2]

My father was one year old when, on May 10, 1933, the Nazis carried out a massive book burning on Opernplatz, not far from his family's apartment. The event has long been understood as one of the most important in Germany's history. Chief among the items the Nazis burned were the contents of the vast archive of the Institut für Sexualwissenschaft (the Institute for Sexual Science), which was at the time the most extensive research collection of queer theory in the world. According to the German American historian George L. Mosse, the institute's Jewish director, Magnus Hirschfeld, "became a constant target of attack" after the book burning: "His own name and that of the Institute for Sexual Science . . . which he founded in 1919, were used as metaphors for sexual perversion, symbols of the threat to bourgeois respectability posed by Weimar Berlin."[3]

The Nazis not only targeted Jewish intellectuals who studied queer perspectives but also sought to eliminate any suggestion that queer life was or could be normal. To do this, they would need to do more than terrorize figures like Hirschfeld—they would need to completely remake the country's education system.

One way that the Nazis worked toward this goal was by encouraging the public to draw a connection between overly permissive educational practices and what they saw as "sexual perversion." During the Weimar era, a small number of German educators had undertaken progressive and experimental reforms, lending students more agency in classrooms, eliminating corporal punishment, and adapting their schools to focus on "individual development, social interaction, and educating students for practical reality"—in other words, training them for participation in civic and democratic life.[4] These reforms were a reaction to the conservative nationalist educational model of pre–World War I Germany, which had been designed principally to support German military conquest under emperor Kaiser Wilhem II, which was still dominant in the Weimar era.

Nevertheless, the Nazis saw even these incremental reforms as an affront, and trained their propaganda machine on the country's education system, seeking to make it even more militaristic and supportive of their nationalist aims. Their campaign of demonization linked progressive educational reforms not only to sexual perversion but also to Marxism, in an effort to draw together traditional social conservatives and wealthy business elites in a coalition against democracy and its institutions.

Educational matters were not a fleeting or insignificant area of focus within Nazi politics. The professed goal of Nazi educational policy was to defend the nation's children from obscenity and "Marxism," but in the Nazi imagination this task was inextricably bound up in a broader narrative of national victimhood that had lingered across much of the population ever since the 1919 Treaty of Versailles, which brought World War I to an end by confiscating about 10 percent of Germany's territory and forcing it to pay reparations.[5]

The aim of the Nazi education system—to transform the country's young people into committed ideologues—was a natural extension of Germany's pre–World War I educational model, which had focused on militarism and German supremacy. Adding Nazi educational practices and ideas to an education system with already strong anti-democratic elements produced an army of Germans willing to die for the fatherland.

What we can see from this example of Nazi Germany, and from studying other instances of fascist movements around the world, is that there are *five major themes of fascist education*:

1. National greatness
2. National purity
3. National innocence
4. Strict gender roles
5. Vilification of the left

These themes are essentially different ways that fascist movements stoke grievances among the dominant group they serve in order to further their aims. In the process, they are careful to eliminate any contradiction of their narrative. This would include, for example, any scholarly research revealing flaws in national myths, any form of education that clearly reveals national guilt, any suggestion that diversity and plurality might be beneficial to society, or that more equitable gender relations might be beneficial, or that the political left is significantly less of a threat than they imagine. In what follows, I will explore the history and conceptual landscape behind these themes, how they are tied together to form fascist ideology, and how they function to undergird and maintain a fascist social form of life.

Fascist social and political movements thrive off a sense of grievance. As we have seen in the discussion of colonialism, the Nazi education system emphasized German loss of lands in the Treaty of Versailles, blaming this loss on Jews (i.e., *national innocence*). According to Nazi propaganda, Jewish people were the source of the mythical "stab in the back" that had caused Germany to lose World War I. The allegation was that social democratic politicians had betrayed the German army by entering into peace negotiations. Germany, therefore, was not to blame for the outcome of the war at all but had instead fallen victim to Jewish betrayal. Thus, all of the punishments the country had endured, particularly the loss of territory in Europe and colonies in Africa, could be traced back to the Jews. The idea that Aryan Germans should seek revenge for this betrayal was a central feature of Nazi propaganda.

The pre-existing German education system that the Nazi government inherited when it took power already contained many of the elements of a fascist education—and it eagerly built upon them. The Nazi education system focused particularly on national greatness, taking Hitler's words in *Mein Kampf* to the extreme: ". . . only those who through school and upbringing learn to know the cultural, economic, and above all the political, greatness of their own fatherland can and will achieve the inner pride in the privilege of being a member of such a people."[6]

This education system, and the propaganda apparatus it

encompassed, especially the Hitler Youth, was responsible for Germany's turn against cosmopolitanism. As the historian Gilmer W. Blackburn notes, "The Nazi success in galvanizing overwhelming national sentiment for the regime's short-term goals appears beyond refutation. German youth, for the most part, proved receptive to simplified heroic legends and to black and white comparisons, and German teachers succumbed just as meekly to Nazi *Gleichschaltung*, or coordination."[7]

In his discussion of education in *Mein Kampf*, Hitler stresses the importance of singling out men of the dominant national group to emphasize their greatness:

> Our educational system lacked the art of picking a few names out of the historical development of our people and making them the common property of the whole German people, thus through knowledge and like enthusiasm tying a uniform, uniting bond around the entire nation. They did not understand how to make the really significant men of our people appear as outstanding heroes in the eyes of the present, to concentrate the general attention on them and thus create a unified mood.[8]

This is of course a common pattern in national textbooks. Edward Eggleston's *A First Book in American History: With Special Reference to the Lives and Deeds of Great Americans*, from 1889, provides several examples of "great men" narratives for young readers. In the introduction, Eggleston writes: "In teaching younger pupils by means of biography, which is the very alphabet of history, we are following a sound principle often forgotten, that primary education should be pursued along the line of the least resistance. Moreover, nothing is more important to the young American than an acquaintance with the careers of the great men of his country."[9] But as Hitler intended it, it is meant to be the foundation of an education in national exceptionalism, as it so often does in the context of the United States. The exceptionalist narrative in American education has been sharpened into the very aim of this education by the Trump movement. In a much-touted speech in September, during the Fall 2020 presidential campaign, then-president Donald Trump introduced the White House Conference on American History with a speech about his educational vision and, by extension, the educational vision of his movement, beginning:

> Our mission is to defend the legacy of America's founding, the virtue of America's heroes, and the nobility of the American character. We must clear away the twisted web of lies in our schools and classrooms, and teach our children the magnificent truth about our country. We want our sons and daughters to know that they are the citizens of the most exceptional nation in the history of the world.[10]

He went on to announce a national commission to promote patriotic education, named "the 1776 commission," and called for restoring patriotic education in schools.

Alongside national greatness is *national purity*, a sense that the nation's identity is defined by the identity of one unified group that exemplifies it. Its most clear-cut example is racial fascism, which considers that group to be a biological race, with distinctive cognitive and physical capacities that make it greater than other races. Religious forms of purity can play similar roles. In the ideology of Hindu fascism, India in the past was a purely Hindu nation. In the ideology of American White Christian Nationalism, the United States is a white Christian country.

With an education system that emphasizes national greatness, and subtly or explicitly some version of national purity, it is then easy to lay the basis for fascism's most powerful political trope. Great Replacement Theory is a name for a type of conspiracy where an internal enemy tries to destroy the nation from within by importing people to "replace" the nation's defining national group. A population raised with myths of national greatness and national purity is particularly susceptible to Great Replacement Theory, as they will believe their nation is great and its greatness is due to the greatness of the defining national group.

In 1916, the American eugenicist Madison Grant published *The Passing of the Great Race*, which decried the supposed replacement of whites in America by Black people and immigrants, including Polish Jews. According to Grant, these groups posed an existential threat to the white race, which Grant saw as America's native population. While Grant did not object to the presence of Black people in America, he insisted that they must be kept subordinate. His book was an exercise in scientific racism, arguing that whites (in his specific and limited sense of Northern European Christians) are superior to all other races intellectually, culturally, and morally, and thus should command a dominant position in society.

Grant tapped into a powerful political current of his time. In the years that followed, the "America First" movement would emerge to oppose internationalism and immigration. In her 2018 book *Behold, America: The Entangled History of "America First" and "The American Dream,"* the historian Sarah Churchwell recounts a February 1921 essay that soon-to-be vice president Calvin Coolidge published in *Good Housekeeping* titled, "Whose Country is This?"[11] In it, Coolidge argued that the United States had become "a dumping ground" and needed to limit immigration to "the right kind"—by which he explicitly meant something like Northern European whites.

It was also in 1921 that the second iteration of the Ku Klux Klan, which began in the early twentieth century, adopted "America First" as part of its official credo. With its fevered commitment to white supremacy and traditional gender roles, the second Klan focused its efforts on spreading paranoia about "Jewish Marxists" and their attempts to use labor unions to promote racial equality. Meanwhile, the American industrialist Henry Ford had been financing the publication and distribution of *The International Jew*, a compilation of articles that claimed Jews were controlling the American media and cultural institutions as part of a global conspiracy to destroy the American nation.

Great Replacement Theory played a central role in Nazi propaganda in Germany, and originally, perhaps *the* central role. In *Mein Kampf*, Hitler was obsessed by foreign immigration and the threat it supposedly posed to the purity of the German nation, writing about the city of Vienna, "I was repelled by the conglomeration of races which the capital showed me, repelled by this whole mixture of Czechs, Poles, Hungarians, Ruthenians, Serbs, and Croats, and everywhere, the eternal mushroom of humanity—Jews and more Jews."[12] According to Nazi propaganda, Jewish betrayal of Germany in World War I was only the beginning of a larger scheme to destroy the Aryan race. As Hitler had it, Jews were members of a foreign race who had become assimilated in Austria and Germany in order to seize control, spreading an ideology of liberalism and human equality to bring about the destruction of Aryans. According to Hitler, "[h]istorical experience . . . shows with terrifying clarity that in every mingling of Aryan blood with that of lower peoples the result was the end of the cultured people."[13] The Jewish destruction of Aryans, he claimed, would be achieved by, for example, gaining control of the press, spreading the doctrine of human equality, using it to justify intermarriage, and encouraging policies that would bring in large numbers of non-whites.[14] In *Mein Kampf* Hitler writes:

> With satanic joy in his face, the black-haired Jewish youth lurks in wait for the unsuspecting girl whom he defiles with his blood, thus stealing her from her people. With every means he tries to destroy the racial foundations of the people he has set out to subjugate. Just as he himself systematically ruins women and girls, he does not shrink back from pulling down the blood barriers for others, even on a large scale. It was and it is Jews who bring the Negroes into the Rhineland, always with the same secret thought and clear aim of ruining the hated white race by the necessarily resulting bastardization, throwing it down from its cultural and political height, and himself rising to be its master.[15]

A similar preoccupation with replacement can be seen in fascist Italy, where that country's dictator Benito Mussolini spread racial paranoia about the decline and replacement of the "white race." In 1934, Mussolini wrote that defending the white race was a "matter of life or death" given "the progress in number and expansion of the yellow and black races."

Great Replacement Theory has proven time and again to be a motivator for mass killing. This is true both of historical incidents of ethnic cleansing and genocide and of contemporary examples, such as the series of mass killing by people not affiliated with a state, carried out mostly during the 2010s and '20s—in some cases by murderers who self-identify as fascist. According to this specific iteration of Great Replacement Theory, known as the *White* Replacement Theory, global elites seeking to diminish the power of white people have enabled the mass immigration of supposedly "high-fertility" minorities.

Since 2011, this version of Great Replacement Theory has been the explicit motivation for the murder of over 160 people in such killings, including Anders Breivik's 2011 slaughter of seventy-seven people in Norway; Dylan Roof's mass murder of Black churchgoers in Charleston, South Carolina, in 2015; the Tree of Life synagogue killings in 2018; the murder of twenty-three people, most of whom were immigrants, at a store in El Paso, Texas, in 2019; and the mass murder of ten Black people in a supermarket in Buffalo, New York, in 2022, also by a White Replacement Theory–obsessed young white man.

In Nazi ideology, it was Jewish people who were behind the plot to replace Germany's Aryan population with non-Aryans (both the 2022 Buffalo supermarket killer and the Tree of Life synagogue killer believed Jews were behind white replacement). We have a great deal of historical evidence, both from European fascism and, more recently, from mass killings, that targeting a group of people as internal enemies responsible for replacing the nation by immigrants is dangerous to them (as well as to those supposedly doing the replacing, the "replacers"). In the United States, Donald Trump has consistently made Great Replacement Theory a theme of his presidential campaigns and his administration, blaming the plot not on Jews, but on his political opponents and Democrats more generally. According to this ideology, his political opposition, the Democrats, are secret Marxists who seek to open the borders to non-white immigration, thereby displacing the white race numerically, culturally, and politically, using the results to place themselves in perpetual power. This is precisely what Hitler claimed about the Jews.

✦ ✦ ✦

Whereas fascist education often serves to absolve the nation of its past sins, or simply erase them, the dominant narrative pushed in the United States today takes a slightly different form. According to this account, the country did commit significant national sins—particularly its perpetuation of chattel slavery. But the seeds to overcome these sins lay in America's founding documents, written by heroic white men—the founding fathers—whose visionary plan for the country charted a path not just to America's absolution but also to its unique world-historical greatness. Slavery, according to this myth, was stamped out by a white man, President Abraham Lincoln, together with the heroism of what is typically presented as an entirely white Union Army. Finally, the last vestiges of racism were dispelled by the actions of a singular Black man, Martin Luther King Jr., whose radical ideas are reduced, in this narrative, to a single line from his 1963 "I Have a Dream" speech, which is misinterpreted as a plea for color-blindness.

Of course, the idea that racism has ended in the United States is patently false—but so too is the idea that the country's founding documents provide a basis for absolution. As the historian Greg Grandin explained in a 2020 article, even the country's push for independence from Britain was tied to indigenous dispossession and genocide:

> American revolutionaries might have argued over slavery, and what place unfree labor would have in a republic founded on the ideal of liberty. But there was one thing that nearly all agreed on: the right to move west. British Americans, before their break with London, chafed at what was called the "Proclamation Line." Running along the crest of the Alleghenies, the demarcation was made by the British Crown after its 1763 victory in the Seven Years' War against France, as an effort to sequester white settlers on the Atlantic Coast. With British subjects already moving through

the mountain passes, the policy became a major source of resentment against colonial rule.[16]

As Grandin makes clear, the founders were complex men, with obvious flaws. But instead of faithfully depicting this complexity, US textbooks have often opted to embrace a simpler narrative, representing them in grandiose, hagiographic terms. A description of George Washington from the 1983 edition of the history textbook *The American Pageant* is a characteristic example. Washington, the book recounts, was a "tall, powerfully built, dignified, blue-eyed Virginia planter . . . gifted with outstanding powers of leadership and immense strength of character." Jefferson, according to the book, "regarded farming as essentially ennobling; it kept men away from wicked cities, out in the sunshine and close to the sod—and God." The book has nothing to say here about those who were also supposed to be "ennobled" by agriculture, the enslaved Black Americans whom many of the founders owned and profited from.

The Trump adminstration's 1776 commission report came out in January 2021. Its purpose, in the words of the commission's 2021 report, was to recount:

> . . . the aspirations and actions of the men and women who sought to build America as a shining "city on a hill"—an exemplary nation, one that protects the safety and promotes the happiness of its

people, as an example to be admired and emulated by nations of the world that wish to steer their government toward greater liberty and justice. The record of our founders' striving and the nation they built is our shared inheritance and remains a beacon, as Abraham Lincoln said, "not for one people or one time, but for all people for all time."[17]

The report largely sticks to the standard narrative that superficially acknowledges America's sins but in the same breath declares them preemptively absolved by the unimpeachable egalitarianism of the founding fathers—ignoring the country's responsibility for slavery and indigenous genocide—and by Martin Luther King Jr.'s ostensible advocacy for color-blindness. According to the report, King's demands for equality carried no broader critique of white America:

> In leading the Civil Rights Movement, Martin Luther King, Jr., was aware that other, more revolutionary groups wanted to fight in terms of group identities. In his "I Have a Dream" speech, King rejected hateful stereotyping based on a racialized group identity. The "marvelous new militancy which has engulfed the Negro community must not lead us to distrust all white people," he warned. King refused to define Americans in terms of permanent racialized identities and called on Americans "to lift our nation from the quicksands of racial injustice to the solid rock of brotherhood" and see ourselves as one nation united by a common political creed and commitment to Christian love.[18]

✦ ✦ ✦

Despite the differences between the subtler narrative of innocence offered in the United States today and the more explicit one offered in the past, fascist practices continue to lace through the country's institutions and politics. Fascism, for instance, draws on the powerful emotions of fear and grievance, which are related—a dominant group fears being replaced, and feels aggrieved over the attendant loss of status and power. We can see these clearly at work in the United States, both historically and today. In his 1935 book, *Black Reconstruction in America*, W. E. B. Du Bois explores how white politicians and wealthy elites in the South exploited these emotions to form poor whites into mobs—and ultimately to prevent the emergence of a labor movement based on the clearly aligned interests of poor white people and poor Black people in the South. Crucial to this weapon against a cross-racial mass labor movement were practices and structures that kept Black citizens subordinated even to poor white citizens. Then demagogues, with the support of wealthy backers, could foment panic by dangling the prospect that poor white citizens might lose even these small advantages in society.

A version of this divisive strategy persists today, evident in the structural practices that largely keep poor white Americans relatively better off compared to their Black peers—

stoking white fears of losing that slight edge, and thus frequently dissuading them from forming labor alliances that could drastically improve their lives.

In the United States, the legacies of slavery, Jim Crow, and other large-scale racial injustices live on in different forms. In 1969, the year of my birth, the number of Americans incarcerated in federal and state prisons was just under two hundred thousand; by 2024, there were more than that many just serving life sentences in state prisons.[19] The total number of people serving time in federal and state prisons is now over 1.2 million, and the total incarcerated population (including local jails, juvenile correction facilities, et cetera) is around 1.9 million.[20] The US prison system disproportionally incarcerates Black people in huge numbers. In 2024, the Black population of the United States was 14 percent of its total population, yet 42 percent of its incarcerated population.[21] According to the Prison Policy Initiative's findings on global incarceration rates in 2021, not only does the United States have "the highest incarceration rate in the world," but also "every single U.S. state incarcerates more people per capita than virtually any independent democracy on earth."[22] The system is bad for everyone but falls particularly harshly on America's population of 48 million Black Americans.

In addition to this, the United States has frequently hindered Black citizens' ability to exercise their right to vote. Unlike in many other democracies, the vast majority of US states (a total of forty-eight) do not allow incarcerated people to vote—and given the criminal justice system's disproportionate impact on Black people, this means that they are significantly likelier than whites to lose their voting rights. In Florida, the current Republican governor, Ron DeSantis, has even created an election police force to address a nonexistent epidemic of voter fraud—and, in the run-up to the 2022 midterm elections, announced the arrests of twenty people on charges of voter fraud, which potentially carried penalties of years in prison. Of the twenty arrested, at least thirteen were Black, and all had been under the impression that they were registering or voting legally. All of this is on top of DeSantis's broader legal attacks on efforts to register more Black voters, which have included instituting an ever more complex set of requirements for voter registration groups—and drastically increasing the fines such groups can face for violating them.[23] What the United States is experiencing today is a return of Jim Crow practices designed to intimidate Black citizens and voters from taking part in public life. Unlike the Third Reich, the Jim Crow regime was never resoundingly defeated and dismantled. Instead, its practices have quietly persisted in varying forms, and while they have sometimes faced setbacks and obstacles over the years, such as the 1965 Voting Rights Act, those obstacles have frequently proven impermanent or surmountable. The Voting Rights Act, for example, has been largely gutted by a series of Supreme Court decisions, beginning in 2013 with *Shelby County v. Holder*.[24] In most cases, racist laws, past and present, are made to appear racially neutral—poll taxes, for example, were widely used in the Jim Crow South, as a way to disenfranchise Black citizens, since many were unable to afford such a tax.

In November 2018, Florida voters approved Amendment 4, which overturned Florida's strict felon disenfranchisement law. In July 2019, Governor Ron DeSantis signed a bill passed by the Florida legislature requiring those with a former felony conviction to pay all their outstanding court fines and fees before regaining the right to vote. In effect, this is a poll tax that continues the disenfranchisement of the very citizens Florida's population voted overwhelmingly to grant back their right to vote. We must understand the assault on education systems in the United States in the same way—as an attempt to return US education to Jim Crow practices.

In the United States, bans on teaching concepts such as critical race theory and structural racism invariably serve to bolster fascist politics. Without an understanding of structural racism, of the practices that maintain racial hierarchies (for example in the carceral system), a white observer may struggle to see the intolerable conditions that drive political movements like the 2020 Black Lives Matter protests. To such an observer, the protests may seem frightening, driven by unfounded anger, the result of a kind of mental instability—and thus a dangerous movement that warrants a violent, characteristically fascist response.[25]

✦ ✦ ✦

Because fascists fear a Great Replacement in which undeserving minorities infiltrate the country and then multiply until they become numerically dominant, procreation and the sanctity of motherhood are central elements in fascist ideology. The role of women is to keep up the numerical advantage of the dominant group in the face of the supposedly "high-fertility" minority groups that stand to "outbreed" them. Thus, fascism tends to elicit panic about low fertility rates in the dominant racial group, and in turn emphasizes strict gender roles. Doing so helps fascist movements to attract the support of two key constituencies—men who feel undermined by shifting gender roles and social conservatives who seek to uphold long-standing patriarchal hierarchies. Ultimately, the defense of strict gender roles can be seen as inherently antidemocratic, in tension with the democratic values of equality and freedom.

We can see this, for instance, in Weimar-era Germany, which experienced a flowering of women's rights. Claudia Koonz, one of the great US historians of Nazism, writes:

As material well-being returned, many Germans, especially the young, felt liberated from the legacy of monarchism and war. The quintessential symbol for the new freedom was the New Woman—youthful, educated, employed, socially free and autonomous. After the war had broken many stereotypes about feminine weakness, popular culture celebrated sexual liberation, and the Constitution granted equality between men and women in the 1920s, social life opened up vistas of freedom.[26]

The Nazis took the Weimar Republic's "New Woman" as a target in their propaganda and policies. Hitler spelled out his regime's views on women's proper roles in society during a September 1934 speech to the National Socialist Women's League:

> The slogan "Emancipation of women" was invented by Jewish intellectuals and its content was formed by the same spirit. In the really good times of German life the German woman had no need to emancipate herself. She possessed exactly what nature had necessarily given her to administer and preserve; just as the man in his good times had no need to fear that he would be ousted from his position in relation to the woman. . . .
>
> If the man's world is said to be the State, his struggle, his readiness to devote his powers to the service of the community, then it may perhaps be said that the woman's is a smaller world. For her world is her husband, her family, her children, and her home. But what would become of the greater world if there were

no one to tend and care for the smaller one? How could the greater world survive if there were no one to make the cares of the smaller world the content of their lives? No, the greater world is built on the foundation of this smaller world. This great world cannot survive if the smaller world is not stable. Providence has entrusted to the woman the cares of that world which is her very own, and only on the basis of this smaller world can the man's world be formed and built up. The two worlds are not antagonistic. They complement each other, they belong together just as man and woman belong together.[27]

Nazi educational policy reflected this vision, providing different tracks for boys' and girls' education. Girls' education included, for instance, fables and stories that glorified motherhood and rural life and overlapped with the existing, socially conservative curriculum that Weimar progressive educators had contested. Ultimately, Nazi girls' education trained women for work in the home, and placed severe restrictions on university education.

The Nazi regime also fomented panic about women's rights more broadly, including birth control and abortion. The Nazis regarded abortion as murder, and hence were staunchly "pro-life," in current terminology. Their defense of life was selective, of course, and did not extend to non-Aryans or disabled Aryans, so they were supportive of abortion for these populations, as they were supportive of murder for these populations. However, abortion for healthy Aryan women was strictly illegal and rigorously enforced. The Nazis linked the obsession with birthrates to the danger that they felt LGBTQ people posed, representing both the "New Woman" and LGBTQ persons as existential threats to the institution of traditional marriage and indeed to Western civilization itself. Nazi officials were so concerned about these issues that in 1936 they established a ministry entirely dedicated to them, the Reich Central Office for the Combating of Homosexuality and Abortion.

Though Italian fascism started out with a more nuanced relationship toward feminism, it quickly aligned itself with the defense of strict gender roles. The historian Victoria de Grazia writes:

> In the New Italy, true men proved their virility by . . . seeding numerous offspring. A punitive tax on male celibacy passed with royal decree-law number 2132, on December 19, 1926, was among Mussolini's very first pronatalist measures. In the penal code of 1931, homosexual acts among men were outlawed. Civil servants were repeatedly enjoined to marry, and after 1937 marriage and numbers of children became criteria of preferment for government careers. . . . For Italian women especially, the Ascension Day Speech, with its emphasis on increasing the birth rate, signaled a turning point in national sexual politics. Still-cherished illusions about the possibility of playing an activist role in the new order were dashed. . . . Above all, motherhood lost the special social meanings that

almost all Italian feminists had invoked. . . . Women's procreative role now potentially defined every aspect of their social being. Thus, Italian women were not only confronted with their exclusion from politics . . . but they also risked exclusion from the entire public sphere: their rights in the workplace, their contributions to culture, and their service as volunteers were all called into question by the official message that their preeminent duty was to bear the nation's children. Worst of all, state authority now embarked on institutionalizing this narrowly cast vision of female roles.[28]

The fixation on gender roles can also be seen in US fascist movements such as the KKK. The Klan's initial incarnation in the late nineteenth century, known as the first Klan, lacked female representation. But by the height of the second Klan's popularity, in the 1920s, an auxiliary branch of the organization had been formed specifically for women, known as the Women of the KKK, or WKKK. The organization represented an idiosyncratic combination of priorities, defending women's suffrage but also spreading paranoid fears that Black men were waiting around every corner to rape white women. According to both the KKK and the WKKK, one of the Klan's primary responsibilities was to preserve the innocence of white women from the depredations of Black would-be rapists. Its purpose in doing so, as in the case of fascist Germany and Italy, was to ensure the continuing production of babies of the country's dominant group. As the historian Nancy MacLean shows in detail, the second Klan also represented themselves as the defenders of the traditional family against changing gender roles.[29]

Today the radical right continues the past fascist obsession with strict gender roles. However, as the Dartmouth historian Udi Greenberg has pointed out, there are important differences between fascist conceptions of gender roles in the 1920s and '30s and the ones present in today's fascist movements.[30] In Nazi ideology, motherhood was incompatible with work—mothers were to stay in the home. There are people who regard themselves as fascist today who embrace this, endorsing online trends such as the "tradwife," a reinvention of the "traditional wife," who works as a homemaker rather than pursuing a career. But there are also contemporary far-right movements that regard motherhood as fully consistent with work. Multiple far-right European parties even have women leaders (and Italy's far-right prime minister, Giorgia Meloni, is female). This would have been anathema in Nazi Germany. In these movements, the goal is to advance childcare programs to encourage considerably larger families without denying women access to the workplace.

Just like the early-twentieth-century fascist movements in Germany, Italy, and the American South, contemporary fascist movements often place great emphasis on promoting traditional heterosexual relationships and traditional marriage while working to marginalize and devalue queer life.[31] It makes sense, then, that these movements would feel threatened by pedagogy that explores the harms of patriarchy or institutional anti-LGBT bias. When far-right politicians and commentators claim that schools are teaching "gender ideology," their aim is to spark a sense of grievance within their socially conservative audiences, and especially to make men feel that their dominant status is at risk, threatened by the encroachment of improperly ambitious women, or "undeserving" queer people. Fascist movements today foment fear among many citizens that if their children learn about critiques of gender normativity, or about the past and present persecution of queer people, those children will not only empathize but also identify with them.

One contemporary observer who has been particularly outspoken about gender roles and falling fertility rates is Allan Carlson, a retired historian at the far-right Hillsdale College in Michigan, who spent much of his career fixated on fertility loss as the cause of Western civilization's decline. What apparently motivated Carlson was his belief that the decadence of Western societies has undermined "the natural family" and led to declining fertility. As the journalist Masha Gessen has documented, Carlson was an influential voice in the development of the ideological basis of contemporary Russian fascism. In the 1990s, following the turmoil of the Soviet Union's collapse, Russia was in the throes of a demographic crisis, which most social scientists blamed on extremely low life expectancies—the country was inarguably suffering from a crisis of mass early death. As Gessen explains in their book *The Future Is History: How Totalitarianism Reclaimed Russia*, Carlson supplied the country's social conservatives with an attractive alternative theory: "Allan Carlson's explanation was entirely different. Russians were dying because what he called the 'natural family' was on the wane."[32] As Gessen describes, Carlson helped found an organization, starting with a conference described as "the World Congress of Families" in Prague in 1997, "dedicated to the fight against gay rights, abortion rights, and gender studies" worldwide, and ultimately spearheaded by Russians. In their book, Gessen goes on to show how the World Congress of Families' socially conservative agenda helped fuel the rise of Russia's current fascist dictator, Vladimir Putin, who since at least 2006 has made the support of "traditional families" central to his program of national renewal.

The influence of Hillsdale College and its faculty—and particularly their focus on social conservatism and strict gender roles—has extended not only to Russia but to other parts of the United States as well. New College of Florida, for instance, was until recently a small, first-rate public institution. But in early 2023, it became part of Florida governor DeSantis's attack on public education in the state, when he appointed six loyalists to the school's board of trustees, in order to institute sweeping changes designed to transform the school into a stronghold for conservatism. A senior DeSantis appointee stated, "It is our hope that New College of Florida will become Florida's classical college, more along the lines of a Hillsdale of the South."

The result of this takeover has been a kind of aggressive masculinization of the student body, with student athletes and a more sports-oriented curriculum given heavy emphasis. According to the American Association of University Professors (AAUP) report on Florida's assault on higher education:

> New College has moved to recruit a large number of student athletes, although until now the school had had no intercollegiate athletics program. Spending lavishly on new "presidential honors scholarships," New College recruited its largest ever first-year class. As of July, New College had 328 incoming students, of whom 115 were athletes. Among that group were seventy freshman baseball players supported by scholarships. By comparison, the University of Florida, an NCAA Division I university with a student body ninety times larger than that of New College, has just thirty-seven baseball players on scholarships. New College also does not yet have a baseball field, or for that matter any other intercollegiate athletic facility, although the parking lot, this committee was told, now has batting cages. As faculty members were quick to point out, moreover, these student-athletes tend to have little interest in either New College's existing liberal arts programs or any proposed "clas-

sical" curriculum. In August, President Corcoran sent a memorandum to faculty members, proposing new majors in finance, communications, and sports psychology, "which will appeal to many of our newly admitted athletes." But, as Amy Reid, a New College professor of French [and faculty chair], commented in the *New York Times*, it is not evident "how sports psychology, finance, and communications fit with a classical liberal arts model."[33]

According to a March 2023 report from the Movement Advancement Project (MAP), a non-profit think tank, titled "Erasing LGBTQ People from Schools and Public Life," the recent "firestorm" of restrictive policies in schools across the United States is part of a concerted effort to demean and diminish LGBTQ youth. As the report describes, the architects of these policies "want to make it impossible for LGBTQ youth to be themselves in schools." They go about doing this by "banning or fining teachers and schools for even talking about LGBTQ people or issues, pulling books off library shelves, and banning teachers from supporting LGBTQ students. In short, they want LGBTQ youth to be treated like they don't exist, and those who disagree will be fired, fined, or even imprisoned."[34]

Bans on LGBTQ literature in schools have been in place in various states for decades, but in many cases they have not been enforced, and over the years they have slowly been removed. As the MAP report makes clear, the United States is experiencing a resurgence of such laws, led by the state of Florida. In March 2022, that state passed what later became known as the "Don't Say Gay" law, which prohibited instruction on or classroom discussion of LGBTQ issues in grades K–3. In April 2023, the Florida Board of Education extended the prohibition through twelfth grade. (In March 2024, however, a legal settlement drastically limited the scope of the law, clarifying that it can apply only to formal classroom instruction.[35] Nevertheless, the law still largely achieved its intended effect, making LGBTQ students and their families feel set apart and devalued.) A number of other states have enacted similar bans on LGBTQ curricula, including Texas, Oklahoma, Louisiana, Mississippi, Alabama, Missouri, Kentucky, Indiana, and Iowa (some of these laws have faced pushback, e.g., in Iowa). Because these laws single out queer people as abnormal and indecent, they not only make LGBTQ children feel ostracized but also teach their peers that they are different and problematic.

LGBTQ citizens make fascism's ideal internal enemy. Like Germany's assimilated Jews, they can appear indistinguishable from other members of the nation. By banning their perspectives from schools and claiming that their very existence is somehow obscene, conservative politicians encourage members of the dominant group to look on them with disgust and contempt. These feelings of intolerance stand in direct opposition to democracy's ideal of freedom, which requires that everyone be free to live as they wish and love who they wish. Fascist movements, therefore, can leverage these feelings to turn citizens against democracy itself.[36]

✦ ✦ ✦

Fascist education and propaganda is harshly anti-leftist, claiming to find Marxists and socialists behind all that is wrong in the nation, especially in its schools and universities. As fascist movements see it, any scholar whose research threatens the myths of national greatness, national innocence, or national purity can be considered a Marxist or a socialist, and therefore a national enemy. Because fascist education is exclusively focused on the glorification of the nation and its dominant group, any history lesson that presents the perspectives of minority populations, or covers social movements such as the labor movement, is antithetical to this project.

These attitudes are clearly evident in contemporary far-right movements in the United States. Hillsdale College, for instance, offers a free online course called The American Left: From Liberalism to Despotism. The course's online description paints a bleak picture of the power and reach of subversive leftist forces:

> American politics has been transformed in recent years as large portions of the federal bureaucracy,

military, the media, and corporate America have embraced the ideas of the 1960s radical Left.

This transformation has brought ideas like transgenderism, identity politics, and global government—which were formerly relegated to the fringes of academia—into the mainstream of American public life. The result of this turn can be seen in the radical gender ideology pushed in our nation's classrooms, the lawlessness at our border and in many of our cities, and the economic policies that continue to hollow out the American middle class.[37]

The course represents leftists as an existential threat to American values, and mainstream liberalism as hopelessly in their thrall. Defeating them, it concluded, is the only way of saving the country.

We see the use of "Marxism" as a shorthand for any education program that conservatives find objectionable in the recent attacks on critical race theory in the United States. Often, these attacks claim that critical race theory is a branch of a nebulously defined field that they call "Cultural Marxism." As the media scholar Moira Weigel pointed out in a recent paper, hardly anyone has ever identified as a "cultural Marxist"—the expression is almost always used pejoratively.[38] The conservatives who use the label seem to think of it as referring to a program that calls for using Marxist tools to destroy "Western civilization" from within, by elevating minority perspectives in schools and universities. Just as in

Nazi propaganda, this plan is said to have been hatched by a group of primarily Jewish intellectuals (in this case, the Frankfurt School), whose teachings have supposedly inspired Black Americans to take part in racial warfare. Weigel writes:

> At the same time, by "proving" that cultural Marxism "spawned" CRT, these authors connect CRT to a well-established image of the enemy. Marxism is what Ahmed (2014) calls a "sticky" signifier. It has become charged with feeling through a long history of statements made about it, including the conspiracy theory that Marxism is a plot by Jewish cosmopolitans to convince non-Whites to overthrow White civilization. This idea echoes in narratives about the Frankfurt School inspiring CRT and CRT inspiring the Black Lives Matter movement.

Just as fascist education prepares citizens to be receptive to Great Replacement Theory, it also prepares them to be alert to charges of Marxism, recoiling from any institution, policy or person associated with the ideology. In fascist education, students are trained to regard anything "Marxist" as dangerous, foreign, and disgusting. Thereafter, politicians can use the term strategically to dissuade citizens from joining potentially subversive social or political movements.

✦ ✦ ✦

Fascism is an ideology that is characteristically employed to justify state violence against political opponents such as minority populations, members of labor unions, or anyone suspected of being a Marxist. It is an ideology that suppresses women's rights, forcing them back into the home. It represents LGBT citizens as deviant and criminalizes their representation. And it is used to justify brutal, inhuman treatment of immigrants.

Scholars of fascism often point out that the ideology must have a material basis in order to succeed in any meaningful way—a sharp economic downturn, for example, or an embarrassing defeat in war, or a lost election. It is less commonly remarked upon but equally true that fascism must have an ideological basis as well. Fascist conspiracy theories (for example, of replacement, or of hidden Bolsheviks everywhere) are no doubt effective on a population anxious about their jobs, or brimming with resentment about a humiliating military defeat. But a population raised on narratives of national greatness and national purity will also be susceptible to Great Replacement Theory politics.

There is a continuum between the supremacist nationalism discussed in the previous chapter and fascism. The German education system's long-standing focus on German supremacy, even before the Nazis' rise to power, smoothed the path for that country's turn to fascism. When a country's education system represents that country as exceptional in the world, standing above all nations in its greatness and innocence, it makes that country susceptible to the violent authoritarian ideology of fascism.

5

Anti-education

To review what we have covered thus far, fascist education works by strategically erasing accounts of history and current events that include a diversity of perspectives, narrowing the scope of what can be taught until students are presented with a single viewpoint, which is formulated specifically to justify and perpetuate a hierarchy of value between groups. This narrowing is inconsistent with multi-racial democracy, antithetical to egalitarianism, and carries the possibility of conjuring mass violence.

But this is not the only means by which authoritarian movements attempt to manipulate populations into accepting the supremacy of a single dominant group. They also sometimes employ an even more scorched-earth strategy, destroying any common reality that could serve as the basis for a broad alliance between citizens against power. They seek to accomplish this by destroying the institution of public education itself.

A theme among right-wing politicians in the United States today is that universities, including the cloistered privilege of elite colleges and universities, are hotbeds of various forms of Marxism. And yet many of these same politicians are themselves the products of the Ivy League. Texas senator Ted Cruz attended Princeton University and then Harvard Law School. Florida governor Ron DeSantis attended Yale University (where I teach) and then Harvard Law School. Arkansas senator Tom Cotton attended Harvard University and then Harvard Law School. Ohio senator J. D. Vance attended Yale Law School. Congresswoman Elise Stefanik graduated from Harvard University. Tom Cotton has denounced his alma mater for pursuing "racist and Marxist 'diversity' policies while tolerating antisemitism."[1] Ron DeSantis (speaking of Harvard) said, "[T]here is an intellectual and moral rot on university campuses now."[2] DeSantis has made targeting universities central to his politics. Ted Cruz published a book warning that "cultural Marxism" was taking over education, transforming universities into "Marxist universities."[3] Politicians who have graduated from these universities, indeed fairly recently, have one way or another denounced elite colleges and universities, casting themselves as regular citizens offended by these universities (including Harvard's) supposedly traitorous and anti-American Marxist extremes.

Stefanik's political career no doubt owes a great deal to the benefits and privileges of her education at Harvard, where she served as a student leader in the Harvard Institute of Politics. After graduation, she took a staff position within the George W. Bush administration. And yet she has made attacking higher education, "holding higher education responsible," suddenly into one of her best-known issues.[4]

Israel's 2023 invasion of Gaza was in response to a horrific terrorist attack by Hamas against Israelis on October 7. There are many possible reactions to terrorist massacres. Violent invasions targeting civilian populations do not have a good track record of success. During Israel's invasion of Gaza, it has bombed civilian populations, and set up the conditions for a famine among the Palestinian population of Gaza. In other words, Israel has committed acts that are legitimately considered war crimes, as well acts that are considered genocide according to the United Nations's 1948 Genocide Convention, which "counts deliberately inflicting on the group conditions of life calculated to bring about its physical destruction in whole or in part" as a genocidal act.[5] Unsurprisingly, the Israeli army's actions led to widespread anti-war protests on college campuses across the United States. It is a long-standing custom in American right-wing politics to use campus anti-war protests to attack and delegitimize universities. Ronald Reagan ran for governor of California in 1966 by attacking campus anti-war protests as "rioting" and "anarchy."[6] In a letter written soon after he took office in 1967, Reagan wrote, "How far do we go in tolerating these people & this trash under the excuse of academic freedom & freedom of expression?"[7] The right-wing attack on universities for their campus protests against the 2023 Gaza War is a rote application of this long-standing tactic of representing campus anti-war protests as violent mobs in an effort to delegitimize universities, professors, and students. But it adds to it the claim that the protesting students (even the Jewish ones) are forming violent *anti-Semitic* mobs. This is understandably quite concerning for Americans of all political affiliations.

In a US congressional hearing on the rise of anti-Semitism on college and university campuses in late 2023, during this wave of student activism responding to Israel's war in Gaza, Stefanik targeted Claudine Gay, Mary Elizabeth Magill, and Sally Kornbluth—the presidents of Harvard University, the University of Pennsylvania, and MIT, respectively—with incendiary questions about their universities' policies. After claiming that protesting students' chants of "intifada" were calls for the genocide of Jewish people, a misinterpretation, and a message, that the students clearly rejected, Stefanik asked the three university presidents whether calling for the genocide of Jewish people would constitute harassment at their universities. The three presidents gave legalistic responses, declining to give a definitive answer and saying that it depended on context. They could not honestly have done otherwise—policies governing harassment must, of course, take context into account. But the legalistic answers did not play well as political theater. Soon after the hearing, the president of the University of Pennsylvania was forced to step down.[8]

Building on the momentum generated by this upheaval, a pressure campaign was soon under way to oust Claudine Gay, as well, who also happened to be Harvard's first Black president. Christopher Rufo, the formidable far-right political strategist, accused Gay of unrelated plagiarism, in which she had allegedly copied phrasings from academic papers by other scholars nearly identically in her own work, but not the arguments. The attack was soon joined by a billionaire hedge fund manager and Harvard donor named Bill Ackman.[9] Eventually, the campaign succeeded—Gay resigned in January 2024. In a statement soon after, Stefanik claimed victory and used the occasion to declare the need for a "reckoning" with the "moral decay, intellectual laziness, and dangerous radical groupthink" of the elite universities, including the one that had played such a pivotal role in her own political career. "Our robust Congressional investigation," she said, "will continue to move forward to expose the rot in our most 'prestigious' higher education institutions and deliver accountability to the American people."[10]

Gay had come to her position with impeccable academic credentials and a career trajectory that largely followed the pattern of many other top university presidents. She had previously served as a much-admired Dean of Social Science at

Harvard, then became Dean of the Faculty of Arts and Sciences.[11] Then she was appointed to the presidency in 2023. And though Gay does appear to have copied sentences from academic papers, no one has suggested that the novel ideas in her research were in any way falsified or taken from others, which would be a far more serious offense.[12] For many it appeared that Gay was targeted not out of any concern for academic integrity, but for other reasons, including, or perhaps centrally, because she is Black and had been appointed to lead an institution with an unmatched profile in society.

As Christopher Rufo made clear in an interview with *Politico*, the attack on Claudine Gay was part of a larger assault on the institutions in the United States. "I've run the same playbook on critical race theory, on gender ideology, on DEI bureaucracy," he said. "For the time being, given the structure of our institutions, this is a universal strategy that can be applied by the right to most issues. I think that we've demonstrated that it can be successful."[13] The attacks on Gay follow the same strategy used so effectively by US senator Joseph McCarthy and other Red Scaremongers during the ideological war on American leftists in the 1940s and '50s—relentlessly harassing a select group of high-profile individuals in order to chill dissent on a large scale.

As of this writing, there is no sign that this most recent iteration of the right-wing attack on universities will stop. In April 2024, Columbia University President Minouche Shafik was dragged in front of a congressional committee (whose behavior has come to suspiciously resemble that of the House Un-American Activities Committee of the 1940s and '50s) to confront the same charges of allowing anti-Semitism (i.e., protests against Israel's actions in Gaza) to flourish on Columbia's campus. In response, Shafik capitulated to the committee's attack on her university, agreeing with their spurious charges and promising to crack down. Her testimony to the committee, and her ensuing actions to call in the NYPD to clear out and arrest the protesting students, spurred divestment campaign encampments in campuses across the United States, to which many universities responded with harsh militarized crackdowns on student protestors. The same right-wing forces that have been attacking universities for decades found a weapon they can cynically employ to draw in wealthy donors and others who might not otherwise support their mission to delegitimize universities.

We can see the same sorts of attacks in other countries led by far-right regimes. One of the first steps Narendra Modi's government took when Modi assumed power in 2014 was to target elite universities, "taking steps like filing police complaints against professors who lectured on topics they disliked."[14] Since then, India's universities, public and private, have been subjected to withering attacks on their intellectual autonomy and freedom, primarily surrounding issues of religious tolerance. Devangana Kalita and Natasha Narwal were students in Delhi, and the two founders of the student collective Pinjra Tod, which was formed to advocate against unequal treatment of women and male students at hostels. In 2020, Pinjra Tod was central to organizing peaceful student protests on university campuses against India's Citizenship Amendment Act of 2019, which gave preferential treatment to non-Muslim residents of India for citizenship. In reaction to these peaceful protests, which were falsely represented in the media as part of violent riots in Delhi, the two founders of Pinjra Tod were arrested and imprisoned, charged with incitement to riot, attempted murder, sedition, and a host of other crimes. They are currently out on bail.[15] Universities in India are now closely watched for signs of so-called "anti-Indian" sentiment. These signs include defending liberalism, including defending equal rights for India's Muslim population.

This attack has not spared India's private universities. Pratap Bhanu Mehta is a world-renowned political theorist and a critic of India's ruling party, the Bharatiya Janata Party (BJP), who in 2017 became the vice-chancellor of India's Ashoka University. In 2021, the university's trustees reportedly told him that "his intellectual interventions were something they could no longer protect."[16] As a result, Mehta resigned from his position as vice-chancellor and the faculty. Presumably, supporters of India's autocratic government had found a way of pressuring Ashoka, which is a private university and thus (in theory) not answerable to the government.

Jawaharlal Nehru University is one of the elite universities in India, a liberal intellectual institution like one of the great universities in the United States that graduates a country's intellectual "upper crust." Their professors and students have been harshly targeted by the Hindu Nationalist government and its supporters.[17] This rhetoric has spurred violent mobs to attack its university students on campus. Newly hired Hindu nationalist administrators have suspended students for demonstrations and protests, just as multiple university presidents have now done in the United States. In short, India's Hindu nationalist government is freely destroying its best universities. It is the same process, but further along, as what the United States is experiencing today.

As we have seen, in the United States some of the leading politicians decrying institutions of higher education as factories of leftist indoctrination are often among those who have benefited the most from them. And their peers who have more modest educational backgrounds tend to ignore the fact that the conservative political movement they are part of is largely directed by Ivy League graduates. It strains credulity to believe that the institutions that have produced graduates who count among the most extreme, far-right, and anti-democratic politicians in the country today are engaged in "liberal indoctrination." The facts clearly indicate a different situation. In any country with elite institutions, its graduates constitute something like a ruling class, and in most cases, that ruling class will be composed of people with a diversity of political views. In the United Kingdom, for example, much of its political elite (including those with drastically different ideological leanings) has for centuries been composed of graduates from its privileged secondary schools and its two premier universities, Oxford and Cambridge.

In such countries, power-hungry politicians of different political ideologies will emerge from their top schools eager to acquire and retain positions of influence. For many of them, and especially those whose hostility to the economic interests of ordinary people prevents them from winning popularity on the merits of their ideas, a politics of fake anti-elitism is the surest path to achieving the power they crave. In this light, the hypocrisy of Ivy League–educated Republican politicians makes perfect sense. Elite institutions also give these power-hungry politicians both the skills required to spread their extremist, right-wing, anti-democratic ideology— and, in the case of these particular faux populists, the network and connections to do so effectively.

Like the United Kingdom, the United States has a class structure built around top-tier universities, which grant access to networks of power and wealth. As such, they are perfectly legitimate targets of mass resentment. But their right-wing critics frequently pursue a different line of attack, decrying these institutions as hotbeds of Marxism. In fact, they are antithetical to Marxism, which is, of course, a political philosophy that rejects class hierarchies.

Though I am not a Marxist myself, I feel comfortable saying that no Marxist would support the mission and role of elite universities, nor would Marxists be particularly inclined to teach at one. Contempt of these institutions for their role in promoting and maintaining class hierarchies is itself a Marxist position. When right-wing politicians absurdly link elite universities to egalitarian philosophies like Marxism and socialism, something else is going on. If one looks at what is happening in the best universities in India, one can see a grim but plausible future near term course for America's.

One of the most significant threats that a class hierarchy can face is a universally accessible and excellent public school system. The political philosophy that feels this threat most acutely—and that unites hostility toward public education with support for class hierarchy—is a certain form of right-wing libertarianism, an ideology that sees free markets as the wellspring of human freedom. These kinds of libertarians oppose government regulation and virtually all forms of public goods, including public education. The political goal of this version of libertarian ideology is to dismantle public goods. The dismantling of public education is backed by oligarchs and business elites alike, who see in democracy a threat to their power, and in the taxes required for public goods a threat to their wealth. Public schools are the foundational democratic public good. It is therefore perfectly logical that those who are opposed to democracy, including fascist and fascist-leaning movements, would join forces with right-wing libertarians in undermining the institution of public education entirely.

One of the pioneers of the wave of attacks against public universities in recent years was former Wisconsin governor Scott Walker, who made his mark fighting to undermine his state's renowned public university system. Beginning with his 2010 run for governor and throughout his subsequent political career, which included two terms in that office, as well as a run for US president in 2016, Walker took every opportunity to devalue higher education and make the university system's work more challenging. As the journalist Karin Fischer explained in a 2022 article for the *Chronicle of Higher Education*, titled "A Playbook for Knocking Down Higher Ed," this fight is at the heart of Walker's political ideology:

> Scott Walker . . . was the anti-education governor. Time and again during his two terms, the Wisconsin Republican made the state's colleges, and those who work at them, political foils, criticizing them as wasteful and out of touch, challenging what was taught in their classrooms, and questioning their value. By the time he left office, in 2019, Walker had slashed college

budgets, stripped tenure protections and university autonomy, and proposed to gut the Wisconsin Idea, enshrined in state law, that stresses higher education's importance to the state and society.[18]

Walker's offensive was so successful at the state level, in fact, that it became a model for a national right-wing campaign against higher education, and helped to marshal Republican political power behind that endeavor. As Yale Law School graduate J. D. Vance declared in a speech at the 2021 National Conservatism Conference, repeating former president Richard Nixon's words, "the professors are the enemy."[19]

For the institutions that help coordinate these attacks, the task of undermining education and the assault on democracy are deeply intertwined. According to a 2021 report from *Politico*, Jessica Anderson, who was then the executive director of the Heritage Foundation's advocacy arm, identified critical race theory as "one of the top two issues her group is working on alongside efforts to tighten voting laws."[20] In Project 2025, the blueprint for a potential second Trump administration organized by the Heritage Foundation, a section on the Department of Justice recommends reassigning responsibility for election-related offenses from the Civil Rights Division to the Criminal Division, where they can be more assiduously prosecuted, with potentially far greater consequences to those targeted. The "election related offenses" that the Project 2025 report recommends prosecuting so aggressively are those such as "fraudulent voter registration, including mail-in ballot fraud" (which, it should be noted, has not been documented in any significant numbers anywhere in the country). If enacted, these plans could result in criminal charges being brought against those who do nothing more than participate in a voter registration drive, and could certainly be used to obstruct other programs for expanding access to voting.[21]

The Manhattan Institute, an influential right-wing think tank, has similarly prioritized attacks on public education, sponsoring an initiative on critical race theory led by Christopher Rufo, the strategist who also helped to oust Claudine Gay as the president of Harvard. Rufo developed a doggedly repetitive method of attacking schools and universities by linking them to this frightening-sounding academic theory, whose meaning in their use is completely invented, and using this specious charge to argue that the institutions have abandoned their true purpose of education in favor of a dangerous ideology that threatens the nation.

This strategy appears to be on the rise within Republican circles. By all accounts, Rufo has had a significant hand in shaping the educational agenda of Florida governor Ron DeSantis. In an article from March 2023, the journalist Michael Kruse elaborates on their relationship:

Part mercenary and part emissary, a mix of a think-tank wonk and a social-media troll, Rufo for the last year and a half has been a main source and surrogate for what DeSantis has sought to make his signature—school boards and higher ed, Disney and issues of teaching and tolerance of gender and sexuality, the overarching palette of policies that DeSantis describes as "anti-woke" and that has been the primary political fuel of his post-pandemic ascent.[22]

In his failed campaign for the Republican nomination in the 2024 US presidential election, DeSantis denounced leftist social justice ideology that promotes open borders, secularism, LGBTQ equality, and high crime rates in urban areas. To combat this pernicious influence, DeSantis proposed various restrictions on curricula related to race and social issues, and—in a seeming imitation of Hungary's attack on Central European University—began his assault on New College of Florida, hoping to create a kind of case study for how to dismantle an esteemed academic institution. DeSantis's increasing hostility toward higher education in the state became so concerning to the American Association of University Professors that the organization formed a special committee on Political Interference and Academic Freedom in Florida's Public Higher Education System.[23]

In the report it eventually issued, the committee describes in detail a total right-wing takeover of the governing structure at the heart of public higher education in Florida, the State University System's board of governors, which is responsible for overseeing the state's twelve public universities and a combined total of about 350,000 students, as well as the trustee boards of each university. When filling positions on this seventeen-member body, DeSantis did not even give a pretense of having considered candidates on the basis of their merits—as the AAUP report notes, his appointees have by and large been "former [Republican] political officeholders and professional political operatives." By the time the AAUP report was published, the entire governing structure of the university system was dominated not just by Republicans, but by Republicans loyal to DeSantis. As a result, according to the report, "[t]he board's increasing tendency has been to follow the lead of the governor and his allies in the [Republican] legislative supermajority." The report then quotes a "veteran faculty member at the University of Florida," who remarks that the current members of the board and the trustees are concerned mainly with their relation to the governor, and not the well-being of the university system.[24]

The presidencies of Florida's public universities, too, the report suggests, are being handed out as political favors to loyalists, rather than awarded to candidates with track records of sound management and demonstrated commitment to the integrity of the institution. As one faculty member, the political scientist Sharon Wright Austin, explained to the authors of the report, "The governor does not like criticism or anyone to challenge him. . . . University presidents are not supposed to be puppets, but this is Florida, and it's a new time for academia in our state."[25]

These reports suggest that it is dangerous, as a faculty member at a Florida public university, to be openly critical of DeSantis. By appointing candidates to the board of governors and university presidencies based on loyalty and political favors, DeSantis has simultaneously strengthened his control over the broader Florida political landscape (by gaining another incentive to offer) and heightened his control over the university system. In short, the AAUP report describes a university system in the midst of an authoritarian takeover, standing on the precipice of destruction.[26]

DeSantis's attack on public universities, and education in general, is part of a larger right-wing effort to replace pluralist, democratic forms of education with narrower, ideologically motivated ones better suited to indoctrination. This effort is complemented by another kind of attack on education, which stems not from a fascist impulse to recast the system for its own purposes, but rather from a libertarian impulse to eliminate the system altogether. The end goals of these two camps may be somewhat different, but many of their tactics are the same, and their shared enemy makes them natural allies. For instance, just like Ron DeSantis, many libertarian opponents of public education seek to undermine universities and schools by tying them to concepts they expect the public (and especially the white middle and upper classes that comprise their base) will find frightening and vaguely threatening—concepts like social justice, critical race theory, or structural racism.

Destroying America's public schools and universities, which are perhaps our most important public good, has long been a goal of the libertarian right, though it has frequently taken a gradual, incrementalist approach, disingenuously claiming that measures like voucher programs, which steer tax dollars to private schools, are not intended to destroy the public system but to complement it by offering students and parents "school choice." Frequently, libertarian opponents of public education can be so guarded about their ultimate aims, and more authoritarian opponents can be so blindly hostile to educational institutions, that it is difficult to distinguish between them. Some even seem unclear themselves about which camp they belong to. There are perhaps no better exemplars of this confusion than former president Donald Trump and his secretary of education Betsy DeVos.

For decades before her appointment to lead the US Department of Education, DeVos and her family played a central role in undermining her home state of Michigan's public education system.[27] DeVos's husband, Dick DeVos, who for a time served as president of Amway, the multi-level marketing firm co-founded by his father, was elected to the Michigan State

Board of Education in 1990. DeVos later became a major backer of various anti–public school initiatives, such as voucher programs and tax exemptions for private education, both of which serve to dramatically reduce funding for public schools. The DeVoses are also major funders of the Mackinac Center for Public Policy.[28] The Mackinac Center is a Michigan-based think tank founded in 1987 that has had an enormous influence on the movement to privatize public goods in the state, with education being among the central targets of this mission. But as the journalist Andy Kroll explained in an article for *Mother Jones*, the center's ambitions for privatization extend beyond just education:

> The Mackinac Center is a fervent advocate of privatization—its scholars support outsourcing everything from public school districts to Amtrak to state prisons—and backs anti-union legislation for Michigan. In 2007, the center published "A Collective Bargaining Primer," advocating against mandatory unionization and automatic dues deductions for public school teachers and other public employees. Collective bargaining for teachers, the Center claims, "has become a significant deterrent to educational quality." In other words, if you outsource as much as you can and kneecap the unions, the quality of education—and presumably city services—increases.[29]

The Mackinac Center was also a major source of support for the 2012 expansion of Michigan's emergency management act, which Republican governor Rick Snyder signed into law, allowing him to replace the mayor and city councils of cities found to be in "financial emergency" with "emergency managers," who would have the authority to make decisions on behalf of the city. Under the 2012 expansion of the law, these emergency managers were given unique and extraordinary powers, including the ability to break contracts with unions, sell city assets, and outsource city services. In Flint, Michigan, the first city to come under the auspices of the law after its 2012 revision, emergency managers made a series of decisions that led to that city's devastating water crisis, in which thousands of children were exposed to lead.[30]

It appears from the public political behavior of the DeVos family that tearing down public schools is part of a broader libertarian program that calls for the dissolution of vast swathes of the public sector. Betsy DeVos's brother, Erik Prince, founded the private military company Blackwater, which combines the family's libertarian ethos with a more imperialist bent. Blackwater, which has since been renamed multiple times, made its mark by forging a new model of outsourcing the responsibility for waging war to private companies—which ultimately led to the disastrous Nisour Square Massacre in 2007, in which Blackwater security guards killed seventeen Iraqi civilians in Baghdad.[31] In a 2024 episode of his podcast *Off Leash with Erik Prince*, Prince seemed to advocate the invasion of foreign countries simply on the basis of what he sees as their weaknesses. "If so many of these countries around the world are incapable of governing themselves," he said, "it's time for us to just put the imperial hat back on, to say, we're going to govern those countries . . . cause enough is enough, we're done being invaded. . . . You can say that about pretty much all of Africa, they're incapable of governing themselves."[32]

The Australian sociologist Melinda Cooper has argued persuasively that the marriage between right-wing libertarianism, neoliberalism, and social conservatism is not merely one of convenience.[33] As she shows, some of the major figures of the libertarian movement, including Milton Friedman and Gary Bauer, wished for the deconstruction of public goods in part because they thought that doing so would restore the traditional role of the family. "Neoliberals such as Friedman begin with the self-evidence of individual responsibility," she writes, "but end up affirming the necessity of familial obligations when confronted with the social costs of unwaged dependents."[34] In other words, if there is no state to support citizens in need, they will be obliged to fall back on their families and religious communities for support. This has the effect of reinforcing traditional social values, since it puts these families and communities in a position to condition their support on the rejection of certain beliefs, identities, or ways of life that they may find objectionable. A robust system of public goods gives citizens the necessary support structures to make their own choices—and to take full advantage of democracy's freedoms. And this is exactly why social conservatives and libertarians alike find democratic forms of education so threatening.

It is not essential to implement the full ideological program of a fascist education to dismantle a democratic education system. Simply eliminating the elements that create opportunities for social and economic equality will suffice, leaving behind little more than assertions of national exceptionalism and narrow job training.

The effects of one's education last a lifetime. In my public high school, there was a history teacher who held far-right views, which colored his teaching of the Second World War. Many years later, I happened to notice a classmate of mine who took history from this teacher asserting on social media the outlandish theory that Hitler was part Jewish, which, in his estimation, meant that the Nazi Holocaust was in part an internal Jewish matter. Obviously, many other factors in his life shaped his views and his sense of history, but the role of the history teacher is clear. We can begin to grasp the destructive potential of anti-education if we imagine everyone subject to different versions of that teacher—a massive patchwork of different forms of schooling, ranging from religious indoctrination to bare-bones vocational training with no history at all. No democratic culture can rest upon such an impoverished education. Without a common understanding of reality, and a common sense of history, social and economic equality are impossible.

There are multiple ways to attack democracy through the education system. Fascist education is education for mobilization. Like fascist propaganda, it prepares citizens for violence, in defense of a leader, an ethnic group, or a religion. It creates a sense of aggrievement and resentment that is used to justify violence in support of a leader—whether to gain revenge for a supposed betrayal of the military or a stolen election. It is anti-democratic, hierarchal, and authoritarian. Anti-education, by contrast, is education for demobilization. The goal of anti-education is not only to render a population ignorant of the nation's history and problems but also to fracture those citizens into a multitude of different groups with no possibility of mutual understanding, and hence no possibility of mass unified action. As a consequence, anti-education renders a population apathetic—leaving the task of running the country to others, be they autocrats, plutocrats, or theocrats.

6

Classical Education

I sit with Shakespeare and he winces not. Across the color line I move arm in arm with Balzac and Dumas, where smiling men and welcoming women glide in gilded halls. From out the caves of evening that swing between the strong-limbed earth and the tracery of the stars, I summon Aristotle and Aurelius and what soul I will, and they come all graciously with no scorn nor condescension.

—W. E. B. Du Bois[1]

Canon building is empire building. Canon defense is national defense. Canon debate, whatever the terrain, nature, and range (of criticism, of history, of the history of knowledge, of the definition of language, the universality of aesthetic principles, the sociology of art, the humanistic imagination), is the clash of cultures. And *all* of the interests are vested.

—Toni Morrison[2]

From the hour of their birth, some are marked out for subjection, others for rule.

—Aristotle, *Politics*[3]

As we have explored in previous chapters, the purpose of fascist education is to advance a narrative in which the nation and its dominant group are understood as both superior and innocent.[4] Under such an education system, citizens become vulnerable to fear and resentment, emotions that fascist leaders can easily exploit to maintain and build their power. Yet politicians often advance these systems of indoctrination by claiming to do exactly the opposite, by claiming that they are committed to "freeing schools from indoctrination."

One model of education that is often posited as a corrective to such indoctrinatory systems is classical education, which is to say, a system of education that intentionally forms its canon from the paradigmatic texts of Ancient Greece and Rome, steeping students in their debates and perspectives. Classical education frequently emphasizes, for example, the practice of dialectic, or inquiry by argument, and ideals such as knowledge, justice, virtue, beauty, and truth. It is also sometimes understood to include the major works of the European Enlightenment that laid the basis for liberalism and democratic self-rule—in philosophy, this includes those by John Locke, David Hume, Rousseau, Kant, and others.

Those who see classical education as an antidote to fascist education rest their hopes on its potential to counteract processes of dehumanization, by giving students a sense of meaning and value that is distinctively human. But classical education can itself just as easily be used as a tool to dehumanize, to reinforce hierarchy, to support the supremacy of the dominant group by casting it, and it alone, as the rightful inheritor of the tradition carried forward from the classical civilizations of Greece and Rome to the European Enlightenment, and beyond. Indeed, the far right, both historically and today, has advanced its attacks on democratic education by claiming to promote classical education or the "Western Canon." The Nazis, for instance, were especially enthusiastic proponents. In a section of *Mein Kampf* titled "Value of Humanistic Education," Hitler writes:

> Especially in historical instruction we must not be deterred from the study of antiquity. Roman history correctly conceived in extremely broad outlines is and remains the best mentor, not only for today, but probably for all time. The Hellenic ideal of culture should also remain preserved for us in its exemplary beauty. We must not allow the greater racial community to be torn asunder by the differences of the individual peoples. The struggle that rages today is for very great aims. A culture combining millenniums and embracing Hellenism and Germanism is fighting for its existence.[5]

According to Nazi ideology, the German Empire was the intellectual and spiritual heir of Ancient Greece and Rome, the defender of its traditions. As the historian George Mosse has explained, the Völkisch ideologists who laid the groundwork for Nazi ideology argued in fact that the German people were the *same people* as those responsible for the great civilizational achievements of Ancient Greece and Rome—that "[f]rom the beginning, before they had entered history as a group, Germans had affected the culture of Ancient Greece and Rome. This theoretical assertion transformed the ancient Greeks into Germans and divorced modern Greeks from their classical heritage. Similarly, Rome in its glory period must have been led by Germanic leaders."[6] One sees in this ideology the postulation of a mythic white race, projected backward into history, who are responsible for all of the accomplishments attributed to "the West."

As my father clearly recognized in the British colonial schools in Kenya before independence, the classical Western education he so admired could be twisted, used not to promote critical thinking about ideals, but to assert the superiority of a race, group, or nation.

Across the United States today, far-right politicians and activists advance extreme nationalist programs of education under the guise of "Classical Education," representing America's founders as the rightful successors to the legacies of Ancient Greece and Rome. For example, Hillsdale College, the ultra-conservative Christian college in Michigan, has become deeply involved in efforts to challenge progressive education, proposing classical education as a superior alternative. Their website offers online courses on Edward

Gibbon's *The History of the Decline and Fall of the Roman Empire*, Dante's *Divine Comedy*, and Aristotle's Ethics, alongside courses with titles like "The American Left: From Liberalism to Despotism," "The Great American Story: The Land of Hope," and "Supply-Side Economics and American Prosperity with Arthur Laffer."[7] It offers a history course titled "American Citizenship and Its Decline," which includes a video introduction announcing that the course will show how American citizenship depends on classical conceptions of citizenship and the "visions of our founding fathers," both of which are under threat from "wokeness."[8] The message is clear—a classical education is one that recognizes progressivism as despotism, embraces supply-side economics, and sees America as the inheritor and defender of Western ideals of freedom.

Given its contradictory uses and misuses, we can only conclude that classical education does not have any fixed relationship to hierarchy—it can either reinforce hierarchy or oppose it. Its orientation in this respect depends on whether the classical texts in question are taught as exemplars of their authors' genius and their culture's superiority, or as a means of exploring the ever-relevant ideas and questions raised by these texts. Fascist education systems tend to do the former, while democratic ones tend to do the latter.

✦ ✦ ✦

Though I share some of the common criticisms of "the Western Canon" voiced by those who advocate for expanding the focus of curricula to include the perspectives of varied groups, including members of non-dominant ones, that is beside the point here. I regard the general interest of many classical texts as beyond dispute, and some of the practices and values they posit as potent tools to use in combating certain forms of dehumanization. Classical texts are, by and large, just as relevant today as when they were written. But they are not a basis for any group to think itself superior to others. To see the United States as the descendant of a classical Greek and Roman tradition is to engage in a self-aggrandizing nationalist myth just as the Nazis did.

We must be cautious in transposing any element of classical thought to our own time. There is no uniform set of values or ideals that span this vast stretch of time, much less uniformly positive ones that would be worth unconditionally celebrating as a distinctive national inheritance. We must remember, after all, that classical societies practiced slavery, insisted on the subservience of women, and held many views that we would today find reprehensible.

When taught as a practice of uncritically venerating the authors and societies that produced its great texts, classical education can easily become a justification for colonialism and the "civilization savagism" paradigm on which it rests.[9] In this model, classical education draws a line between the "civilized" societies of Greece, Rome, and their apparent successors, on the one hand, and everyone else on the other. According to the civilization savagism paradigm, the "uncivilized" are not fully human, and may reasonably be reduced to their capacity for labor. Because of this, they are worthy only of what we might call industrial education, a dehumanizing form of education focused entirely on technical training, which ascribes no value at all to knowledge.

But when taught as a practice of critical inquiry and an exploration of concepts like truth, beauty, and justice, classical education leads us to exactly the opposite conclusion: that human value is not reducible to our capacity for work—that, to paraphrase Socrates, humanity's greatest goal is the acquisition of knowledge.[10]

When fascists adopt classical education, then, they rely on the flattened, instrumentalized version of it, which does nothing to challenge the practice of viewing people solely in terms of their productive capacity—in the case of women, the capacity to produce children, and in the case of men, the capacity for labor.[11] The Nazis, for example, who praised the virtues of an education in Western civilization, were also responsible for the mass extermination of disabled people. According to the distinguished historian of Nazism Nikolaus Wachsmann, the main criterion in selecting which disabled people should be gassed was "the patients' ability to work: anyone regarded as unproductive would be killed."[12]

Moreover, fascist appropriation of classical education distorts not only how the texts are taught, but the ideas themselves. In book 1 of Plato's *Republic*, for instance, Thrasymachus argues that justice is whatever is in the interests of the powerful, a position that plainly resonates with Nazi ideology and twentieth-century fascism more broadly.[13] But this is not at all to say that the Nazis' genocidal views have any legitimate basis in classical civilization. Whereas Thrasymachus's claim is about individuals, the Nazi position is about race, a concept that (especially in the biological sense that the Nazis used it) was largely or perhaps even completely absent in the context of Athens in the fifth century BC. Even more importantly, however, much of the remainder of *Republic* is a repudiation of the position Thrasymachus takes in book 1. Socrates systematically argues against the view that *power alone* should guide action. And according to Plato, it is *reason alone* that should guide action. The basic canonical texts of classical education, the works of Plato and Aristotle, urge that reason and virtue should guide action, and not power.

At its best, classical education can be liberatory, a possibility that was readily apparent to many of the twentieth century's most radical figures. Dr. Martin Luther King Jr., for example, when he taught a social philosophy seminar at Morehouse College, devised a final examination that asked students to compare the theories of justice in Plato and Aristotle, evaluate the radical ideas in Plato's *Republic*, and also contained questions on Aquinas, Hobbes, Locke, and Kant. It is very clear that Dr. King regarded classical texts as important for students to engage with.

Classical history, just as much as classical philosophy, provides a source of critical reflection on the concepts of democracy, empire, colonialism, genocide, and tyranny. The Athenian Pericles, in his funeral oration to commemorate all who fell during the first year in the Peloponnesian War, is reported by Thucydides as describing democratic Athens as follows:

> Its administration favors the many instead of the few; this is why it is called a democracy. If we look to the laws, they afford equal justice to all in their private differences; if to social standing, advancement in public life falls to reputation for capacity, class considerations not being allowed to interfere with merit; nor again does poverty bar the way, if a man is able to serve the state, he is not hindered by the obscurity of his condition. . . . We throw open our city to the world, and never by alien acts exclude foreigners from any opportunity of learning or observing . . . while in education, where our rivals from their very cradles by a painful discipline seek after manliness, at Athens we live exactly as we please, and yet are just as ready to encounter every legitimate danger.[14]

In all of these remarks, Pericles brings out what is distinctive and admirable about democracy's ideals, in contrast to rival systems of government. For example, Pericles, as presented by Thucydides, stresses the connection between welcoming foreigners into the city, and the system and culture of democratic governance. This is a value that stands starkly opposed to the harsh xenophobia of fascism.

Cleon, like Pericles, was an Athenian citizen. Unlike Pericles, he regarded democracies as weak, and incapable of carrying out the brutalities required to maintain an empire. In a famous speech responding to the Mytilenean revolt during the Peloponnesian War, he calls for the Athenians to execute not only the revolt's leaders but all Mytilenean men. Colonialism, urges Cleon, requires an uncompromising cruelty that the democratic spirit weakens:

> I have often before now been convinced that a democracy is incapable of empire, and never more so than by your present change of mind in the matter of Mytilene. Fears or plots being unknown to you in your daily relations with each other, you feel just the same with regard to your allies, and never reflect that the mistakes into which you may be led by listening to their appeals, or by giving way to your own compassion, are full of danger to yourselves, and bring you no thanks for your weakness from your allies; entirely forgetting that your empire is a despotism and your subjects disaffected conspirators, whose obedience is insured not by your suicidal concessions, but by the superiority given you by your own strength and not their loyalty.[15]

Cleon's speech, delivered in the fifth century BC, brings out the tensions between and contradictions within colonialism and democracy, and remains ancient history's paradigmatic act of demagoguery. His justification for slaughtering all Mytilenean men consists entirely of his assertion that the Mytileneans would do the same to the Athenians, if their roles were reversed. This justification for genocide has been repeated over and over throughout history, a rhetorical flourish that Susan Benesch and her colleagues at the Dangerous Speech Project have called "accusation in a mirror."[16] But like Thrasymachus's advocacy for prioritizing power above all else, Cleon's murderous perspective, as it is relayed to us by the historian Thucydides, is not correct, but rather a grave warning about the capacities of humans for cruelty in the service of colonial domination.

Far from being an affirmation of modern far-right politics, many of the ideas found in the texts of classical education are deeply challenging to its preconceptions. The far right today, for instance, sees the family as sacrosanct, and attacks ostensibly liberal education systems for teaching subversive ideas, supplanting the role of parents, and even (in the most extreme and outlandish accusations) grooming young children for sexual exploitation. But if today's conservatives are scandalized by public schools and what is taught at universities, they would be more than a little displeased to learn of the educational interventions prescribed in the major works of their beloved Western Canon. In book 5 of *The Republic*, for example, Socrates advocates removing children from their families so they can be educated by the state.[17] Plato's *Symposium* presents homosexual relationships between teachers and their young students as normal and unremarkable.[18]

While the reality of classical education may be far less compatible with far-right political ideologies than their adherents would like to think and classical education has many virtues, its texts are far from fully supportive of modern democratic education, either. Plato was not a fascist, but he was certainly *against democracy*. Many classical texts accept human slavery as ordinary and permissible. Aristotle, in *Politics*, posits the idea of a "natural slave," or a person who is dispositionally inclined toward servility—a concept that has since frequently been used to justify domination and enslavement.

✦   ✦   ✦

What we are left with is that classical texts can support both democracy and fascism, freedom and unfreedom, equality and hierarchy. And these two uses cannot easily be disentangled. Are Greek and Roman conceptions of freedom explicable without the attendant conceptions of slavery? Are Enlightenment conceptions of freedom and the rights of man intelligible without the system of racialized slavery that was dominant at the time? About the founding of the United States, Toni Morrison writes:

> ... the rights of man, an organizing principle upon which the nation was founded, was inevitably, and especially, yoked to Africanism. Its history and origin are permanently allied with another seductive concept—the hierarchy of race. As Orlando Patterson has noted, we should not be surprised that the Enlightenment could accommodate slavery; we should be surprised if it could not. The concept of freedom did not emerge in a vacuum. Nothing highlighted freedom—if it did not in fact create it—like slavery.[19]

Indeed, we see the deep connections between notions of freedom and unfreedom throughout the history of the United States. Take, for instance, the freedom of the American settlers who migrated westward, or the freedom of southern planters and slaveholders. Such conceptions of freedom depend largely on the counterpoint of the unfreedom and subjugation experienced by Black and indigenous people.

We can ask similar questions about the ideals of reason and autonomy. In both the classical and Enlightenment traditions, the full capacity of reason is understood to be available only to men, and only within a favored group (e.g., the Greeks, or white Europeans). In his classic 1997 work, *The Racial Contract*, the philosopher Charles W. Mills summarizes the views of major Enlightenment thinkers toward non-white populations:

> One early seventeenth-century minister characterized Native Americans as "having little of Humanitie but shape, ignorant of Civilitie, of Arts, or Religion; more brutish than the beasts they hunt, more wild and unmanly [than] that unmanned wild Countrey, which they range rather than inhabite; captivated also to Satans tyranny." In later, secular versions, it is a raced incapacity for rationality, abstract thought, cultural development, civilization in general (generating those dark cognitive spaces on Europe's mapping of the world). In philosophy one could trace this common thread through Locke's speculations on the incapacities of primitive minds, David Hume's denial that any other race but whites had created worthwhile civilizations, Kant's thoughts on the rationality differentials between blacks and whites, Voltaire's polygenetic conclusion that blacks were a distinct and less able species, John Stuart Mill's judgment that those races "in their nonage" were fit only for "despotism." The assumption of nonwhite intellectual inferiority was widespread, even if not always tricked out in the pseudoscientific apparatus that Darwinism would later make possible.[20]

Many classical and Enlightenment thinkers had similar views on women's capacity for reason. Take Jean-Jacques Rousseau, for instance—one of the central figures in democratic political philosophy, whose work largely concerns the dangers of inequality. In his 1762 treatise *Émile*, Rousseau describes the type of education necessary to prepare a citizen for democratic life through the narrative of a boy, Émile, who grows into manhood, and the idealized education that guides him to autonomy. In the final chapter, Rousseau lays out a corresponding model of education for girls, contrasting the education of Émile with that of "Sophie." Woman, he writes, "was made specially to please man. . . . If woman is formed to please and to live in subjection, she must render herself agreeable to man instead of provoking his wrath; her strength lies in her charms." Again, the Enlightenment ideals of autonomy and reason are understood to be beyond the capacities of women.

Immanuel Kant, as much as any thinker, deserves to be called the Enlightenment's philosopher, and within his writings we can see these same contradictions. As the art historian Nicole R. Fleetwood writes, aesthetics "was foundational to the development of the liberal citizen subject." But, she continues, for *Kant* this was "a category that excluded enslaved and exploited people, indigenous peoples, colonized peoples, women of all races, and the criminalized. . . . Kant's understanding of aesthetic discernment associates European whiteness with modernity, moral virtue, judgment, and freedom."[21] Perhaps it is possible to disentangle these raced aesthetic ideals from Kant's concept of moral personhood. But the position that the Enlightenment concepts are corrupted in this way is worthy of serious consideration. After all, Kant and other Enlightenment philosophers may have thought in these terms.

As we have seen in chapter 2, which deals with colonialism, Enlightenment ideals can be misused in the service of domination and oppression. All ideals can be misused. But for quite some time, many thinkers have also asked the more challenging question of whether these ideals are problematic in their essence, whether they are, in some sense, fundamentally apt for misuse.

The view that the Enlightenment concepts of freedom, reason, objectivity, autonomy, and beauty are "white" seems absurd to many people today. But it would not have seemed absurd to most Enlightenment philosophers. And regardless of what we think of the ideals themselves, it is foolish to dispute that the *language* of these ideals is charged with racial and gendered resonances. It is furthermore impossible to deny that Enlightenment ideals are *historically* linked, at least *correlated*, to hierarchies of race and gender. It is far from some kind of novel twenty-first-century insight that women have long been associated with emotion, and men with reason. Perhaps this has something to do with the Enlightenment ideals themselves, or perhaps it speaks only to systematic misuse of them. This is a topic that philosophers have discussed at least since the advent of the Enlightenment itself.

Crucial to Christianity and then the Enlightenment was

a broad sense of moral personhood, one that stretched across cultures and time. As Daniel Markovits has pointed out to me, it is possible to read Charles W. Mills, in his book *The Racial Contract*, as arguing that there is something in this particular ideal that lends itself to a particularly brutal form of dehumanization.[22] In Enlightenment thought, personhood, the locus of dignity, is not local to a culture or tradition. However, in this very broad sense of personhood, to be *unpersoned* is then particularly dehumanizing.

The institution of slavery is a relatively ubiquitous feature of human societies. But perhaps there is a distinctive type of dehumanization emerging from the Enlightenment that results in particularly brutal forms of slavery and genocide.[23] Mills, in this reading, is suggesting that we can understand the brutality of the version of slavery that emerged during the Enlightenment by reflection on the very thin notion of Enlightenment personhood. In this form of slavery, the enslaved are regarded as non-persons, even in a very expansive notion of personhood. If so, the Enlightenment ideals of personhood have a central role to play in explaining the brutality of racialized colonialism, and the underlying systems of white supremacy. While I do not myself endorse it, this is a kind of criticism of the Enlightenment ideal of personhood that cannot be dismissed out of hand.

✦   ✦   ✦

Another ideal of Enlightenment thought that can be misused to support systems of hierarchy is the concept of objectivity. As the philosopher Louise Antony has argued, human knowledge is inherently partial, but the ideal of objectivity "suggests that knowledge can and should be impartial—that it is possible for human beings to transcend the limitations of their particular epistemic positions and achieve an epistemic standpoint that would somehow constitute a 'view from nowhere.'"[24]

It is impossible for humans to achieve objectivity in the "view from nowhere" sense. There are vastly more possibilities than any human could consider in justifying a claim, given our temporal, physical, and practical limitations. And yet, such an ideal of objectivity is central to many arguments of today's fascist movements, including their hostility toward schools and universities, which they see as having a far-left bias. The ideal of education, in their account, is *neutrality*, where for them, this means a *far-right* bias.

These attacks are plainly disingenuous. Those who criticize schools and universities on this basis could not be less interested in objectivity or neutrality—rather, they seek to replace the alleged bias with their own. This sort of obvious hypocrisy, however, is not the only problem with the ideal of neutrality, understood as a stance that makes no prior assumptions. There is in fact no coherence to the notion of "perspective-free" inquiry. All inquiry takes a stand—at a minimum, a commitment to logical forms of reasoning and basic assumptions about reality. In many cases, inquiry also makes moral presuppositions. To take an example from the philosopher Judith Jarvis Thomson, it is a moral stance, though presumably one easily presupposed, that torturing babies for fun or profit is wrong. Yet, in a strict sense, this could be construed as bias; it is taking a stand on a view without argument. Even clearly political stances are widely assumed in many education systems, and rightfully so—the view that democracy is good and totalitarianism is bad, for example, is often a presupposition in schools in liberal democratic societies.

All education presupposes values, even substantive moral and political ones. The idea that it should not presuppose perspectives, even value-laden ones, involves a false conception of objectivity, and a tendentious and in fact ultimately incoherent distinction between facts and values. All inquiry must make presuppositions, and these presuppositions form an intertangled web of fact and value. The demand for neutral inquiry is philosophically incoherent.[25] No wonder that such demands invariably, and hypocritically, mask political agendas.

✦　✦　✦

As the example of neutrality shows, the ideals of the classical world and the Enlightenment can easily be misused, but their misuse sometimes also points to a deeper flaw. In some cases, these are simply bad ideals. The ideal of the "view from nowhere"—that humans can be perfectly neutral or objective—is both false and the basis for cynical attacks on education. The reason it can be used in this way is inseparable from its falseness. This raises the question: Are other classical and Enlightenment ideals similarly flawed? The ideals of autonomy, reason, liberty, and equality are also frequently misused. Does this mean that they, too, are bad ideals?

Many of today's right-wing proponents of classical education feel that the great civilizations on which such an education is based and their uniquely brilliant contributions have come under threat only recently at the hands of myopic academics whose dogmatic focus on oppression and the marginalized leads them to discard these invaluable ideas. But challenges to classical and Enlightenment ideals are nothing new. Indeed, as we saw in chapter 3, Enlightenment ideals have been the subject of criticism for nearly as long as they have been around. The "counter-Enlightenment" philosopher Johann Gottfried von Herder, for instance, rejected many of his peers' ideas, including their assertion of a universal standard of civilizational progress, which he correctly sensed could serve as a justification for brutal colonial subjugation. As Herder saw it, each civilization possesses a unique and incomparable character—meaning that there is simply no such thing as universal objectivity, universal reason, or a universal concept of personhood.

The idea that we should reconsider our veneration of classical and Enlightenment ideals is not a modern fad but a tradition that stretches back hundreds of years. It is also one that runs counter to the type of classical education pushed for today by fascists and other members of the far right, in which the texts that comprise its curricula serve mainly as evidence of their authors' genius and their culture's superiority. Indeed, this was exactly the point of the civilization savagism paradigm that Europeans used as a justification for their brutal colonialism. Classical education, today's fascists contend, is vital because it highlights the texts and accomplishments of supposedly superior and distinctive civilizations, from Greece and Rome through to the United States.

Whether Enlightenment ideals of reason, rationality, and progress can be separated from the beliefs of racial and religious supremacy by which they were originally accompanied is not a problem that can be obviously solved. Enlightenment ideals are not sacrosanct in debate; even by their own lights, they can be challenged (in critical inquiry and dialectic). Debates over the meaning and status of Enlightenment ideals are not the result of overzealous academics whose interest in the oppressed and marginalized has led them to sour on European thought, but part of a long philosophical tradition that includes the Enlightenment itself. If these discussions remain alive only in academic departments that study various forms of oppression, such as gender studies or ethnic studies, this simply demonstrates that faculty in these departments are the successors of this lengthy intellectual tradition.

I myself endorse some version of the liberal tradition, and hence some version of Enlightenment ideals such as objectivity, reason, equality, and freedom. As I see it, critiques of these ideals force us to confront the multiple ways they can be understood. Like the philosopher Charles W. Mills, I accept the ideals, but believe we face a legitimate and important question as to which *understandings* of these ideals to adopt.[26]

Many people today assume that the current liberal consensus rests upon a single, continuous intellectual and cultural tradition passed down through classical education. But this is questionable at best. It is true that questions about the nature of justice, rationality, and the good have been discussed continuously from the time of the ancient Greeks through to present-day philosophy departments. But have each of these ideas truly had a stable meaning over the centuries, or have they gradually transformed according to historical particularities and social structures?[27] Perhaps what we see in the history of Western philosophy and religion is not a single discussion of justice and the good that propels us to contemporary liberalism but, rather, many distinct traditions, each with their own peculiarities.

If classical education can act as a bulwark against fascism, its best chance for doing so is not through its ideals and content, but through the practices that structure its pursuit—including what we sometimes call critical thinking, which at its root is inimical to the anti-intellectualism of fascism. But even critical thinking is not a panacea against fascism—some of the twentieth century's greatest thinkers, including the philosopher Martin Heidegger, were fascists. One can, after all, provide a philosophical argument for prizing will over intellect.

As noted earlier, fascist appropriations of classical education tend to focus on the veneration of the cultural and intellectual products of Ancient Greece and Rome as evidence for the greatness of these civilizations—as well as what are deemed to be their successors. In Nazi Germany, for example, the veneration of the Greek and Roman tradition through classical education became an assertion of German greatness, since German fascists saw themselves as the inheritors of these civilizations.

In the United States today, classical education is frequently appropriated in this same way, held up as confirmation of the superiority of European civilization, and of America's status as the unique inheritor of this tradition, expressed in the nation's founding documents, economic system, and conservative social values. It is part of a narrative of a continued line of white greatness, from a Germanized vision of Ancient Greece, through the European "Dawn of Reason" and "Age of Exploration," to the founding fathers (and their plantations). The far-right advocates of classical education use the label as a weapon, seeking to give legitimacy to their anti-democratic agenda.

Fascist education systems use classical traditions to assert the greatness of their nations, which serve as an archetypal, universal ideal. But as Johann Gottfried von Herder knew, such universalism can have violent, destructive consequences. As my father recognized to his dismay in Kenya, classical education can be used to justify the crimes of colonialism. The education he witnessed within the British-run schools there represented the local population as lacking history or agency. Most problematically, it imposed outside systems of value on African society—such as Christianity and private ownership of land—on the clearly incorrect grounds that they were universal Enlightenment ideals, applicable everywhere.

As we have seen, singling out a "classical tradition" and making it the focus of an entire program of education tends to end up supporting a hierarchy of civilization in which some groups and nations understand themselves as superior to others. If the United States is the rightful inheritor of the classical tradition and the classical tradition consists of a set of debates that leads inexorably to the ideals of the US Constitution, then the United States can justify its domination of international affairs with the claim that it is spreading "Western values," a universal good, to places where they are needed. The veneration of the "classical tradition" undergirds the "civilizing" mission of colonialism, under the banner of religion and trade, liberalism, and capitalism.

7

Reclaiming History

The Russian organization known as Memorial was a combination of human rights organization, historical research team, and advocacy group focused on making public education include Stalin's crimes. Memorial was also involved in setting up memorial sites to honor Stalin's victims and encouraging historical research to learn more about them. Yuri Dmitriev, one of the major figures of Memorial, was in charge of its branch in the Karelia region, near the border with Finland. Dmitriev is most famous for his historical research on Sandarmokh, a forest in Karelia where Stalin disposed of the bodies of thousands of Soviet citizens in 1937 and 1938. The nexus represented by Memorial demonstrates the connection between historical memory and human rights. For their work, Memorial won the 2022 Nobel Peace Prize.[1]

The Russian government, however, viewed Memorial's work as subversive, and targeted the organization ruthlessly. In 2014, the Russian Ministry of Justice labeled the organization a foreign agent. In 2016, Yuri Dmitriev was arrested on charges of child pornography for nude pictures of his young daughter that authorities found on his computer, which expert witnesses later demonstrated were taken to monitor a medical condition. Despite being acquitted, Dmitriev was ultimately recharged and imprisoned, and his sentence was arbitrarily extended multiple times to a total of fifteen years.[2] Finally, in December 2021, the Russian government shut Memorial down. Even though the current Russian government is clearly distinct from Stalin's communist dictatorship, the regime definitely finds any historical research into the crimes of their predecessor profoundly threatening.

The fate of Memorial is a case study of what can transpire when authoritarian governments take issue with projects to reclaim and call attention to a country's problematic history. Though memorializing Stalin's victims is not a direct expression of hostility toward Russian president Vladimir Putin and his current authoritarian government, doing so nevertheless contradicts the mythic past on which his project rests, in which the Soviet Union was a manifestation of the great Russian Empire, which was wronged by a decadent West. And perhaps most importantly, calling attention to Stalin's crimes opens the door to scrutinizing the wrongdoing of leaders in general, including Putin.

Russia is not unique in this respect. Authoritarian governments and movements characteristically respond with quick and decisive action to crush any attempts to reclaim less-than-flattering history. At the same time, authoritarian regimes take part in their own, very different kind of historical reclamation, restoring the reputations of once-disgraced figures, and representing the nation's past murderers, fascists, and enslavers as national heroes. These, however, are not genuine attempts to restore history so much as they are cynical attempts to rewrite history for self-serving reasons. To represent Hungarian fascists as a national heroes, for example, is to erase their alliances with Nazis, or their anti-Semitic actions. To represent George Washington as a mythic, unambiguously virtuous founding figure is to erase his role as an enslaver of his fellow human beings. Authoritarian "reclamations" of history are virtually by necessity also erasures of vital historical information for understanding a nation's past.

In the United States, there is a long history in the Black American tradition of reclaiming history. In 1841, James W. C. Pennington, a freedom seeker and the first known Black person to attend Yale University, published the textbook *The Origin and History of the Colored People*.[3] It is a systematic attack on the claims supporting American chattel slavery. The first chapter is a critique of the religious basis of slavery, which holds that Black people are descendants of Ham, the son of Noah in the book of Genesis, whom Noah curses, relegating his successors (in the interpretation of slavery's defenders) to permanent slavery. In the second and third chapters, Pennington argues that Africa has a long and distinguished history of empire and civilization, which in fact pre-dates Europe's. Chapter 6 argues that the idea that Black people are inferior to whites "is not only false but absurd, and therefore ought to be abandoned," supporting the claim with a list of highly accomplished Black people, such as the eighteenth-century philosopher Anton Wilhelm Amo, a Ghanian who received his PhD at the German University of Wittenberg and went on to become a respected professor of philosophy (his work is still studied today).[4] As the Harvard historian Jarvis Givens writes, Pennington's work "inaugurated this tradition, a formalized practice of black people striving to rewrite the epistemological order, challenging the antiblack foundations of the known world."[5]

Nevertheless, despite interventions such as Pennington's, the white supremacist quest to prove the cognitive superiority of white people over Black people has been a persistent force throughout recent history—and continues to this day. One area where it has manifested with particular frequency in recent years has been in the dismissal of Black scholars in elite universities as "DEI hires"—which implicitly could easily be taken as suggesting that they could only have achieved their status because of an unfair advantage. The project has also included dubious scientific arguments, which are as unpersuasive as ever, relying on implausibly minimizing or simply ignoring the *effects* of racism (downstream or immediate) on Black populations living in majority-white countries.

One of the most important works in the battle to reclaim Black history was written by the sociologist, historian, and philosopher W. E. B. Du Bois, responding to the efforts of white historians and politicians to distort Americans' understanding of the Reconstruction period—an ambitious campaign of misinformation waged long before the examples that are most familiar today, such as Germany under Hitler or the USSR under Stalin. This 1935 book, *Black Reconstruction in America*, was intended to correct certain erasures and misrepresentations of history that were dominant at the time, and undergirded a narrative of white innocence and Black inferiority and dysfunction.

This narrative blamed Black Americans in the South for their own adverse circumstances by claiming that they had squandered the limited freedom and autonomy they were granted during Reconstruction. But in reality, of course, they were simply the victims of a brutal white supremacist regime, which directed wave after wave of white racial terror at them, much of it through the first Klan. For various reasons, primarily financial self-interest, white officials in the North chose to look the other way. (Though of course, it was hardly the case that racism disappeared in the North with the end of the Civil War.) In any case, blaming the demise of Reconstruction on its victims served the ideological function of protecting the myth of white national innocence, even in the face of the violence of the KKK, and was used as a central justification for the racial fascism of the Jim Crow regime.

In his book, Du Bois rebuts the claims of white commentators such as W. E. Woodward, a biographer of Ulysses S. Grant, who wrote: "The American Negroes are the only people in the history of the world, as far as I know, that ever became free without any effort of their own."[6] Du Bois shows that enslaved Americans freed themselves, writing:

> It was not the Abolitionist alone who freed the slaves. The Abolitionists never had a real majority of the people of the United States back of them. Freedom for the slave was the logical result of a crazy attempt to wage war in the midst of four million black slaves, and trying the while sublimely to ignore the interests of those slaves in the outcome of the fighting. Yes, these slaves had enormous power in their hands. Simply by stopping work, they could threaten the Confederacy with starvation. By walking into Federal camps, they showed to doubting Northerners the easy possibility of using them as servants, as farmers, and as spies, and finally, as fighting soldiers . . . it was the fugitive slave who made the slaveholders face the alternative of surrendering to the North, or to the Negroes.[7]

Du Bois acknowledges that much has been accomplished in the movement toward racial justice through cross-racial alliances between white abolitionists and Black people fighting for their own autonomy. But even those white abolitionists have not always done the same, and have in fact frequently minimized the role of the formerly enslaved in this fight. Du Bois also shows that Black Americans were central to winning the Civil War—and how they played a vital role in the founding of public schools in the South. Throughout the work, he systematically dismantles the myth that Black political leaders during Reconstruction were corrupt, which was for so long central to the official history of the era.

Pernicious myths, however, embed themselves in history. The persistent effects of the racist myth that Black politicians during Reconstruction were incompetent and corrupt continue to shape the way people think about events in America. We can see the lingering effects of the myths even in our contemporary politics. Former president Donald Trump, for example, blamed his loss in the 2020 elections on corruption in cities, such as Atlanta and Milwaukee, that had either large Black populations or Black leaders. In 2024, after a large container ship slammed into the Francis Scott Key Bridge in Baltimore, some right-wing commentators blamed the incident on Baltimore's mayor, Brandon Scott, whom they disparaged as a "DEI mayor," clearly echoing the racist myths that led to the end of Reconstruction and the rise of Jim Crow.[8]

The struggle to teach the perspective of Black Americans against a system that insists on white greatness and white innocence runs throughout the history of the United States. We have seen that school textbooks in the Jim Crow South represented slavery as a benevolently paternalistic system, and enslaved Black Americans as largely content with its practices. For many decades, white politicians and other officials have fought efforts to include the perspectives of Black Americans in school curricula, motivated by the discomfort of white parents, who have argued that such history embarrasses and shames their children for the misdeeds of past generations. And of course, the efforts to racially integrate public schools, which came to national prominence with the Supreme Court's 1954 ruling in *Brown v. Board of Education*, sparked fierce resistance in both the South and the North.

In *Black Reconstruction in America*, while addressing the US education system and the uncomfortableness white Americans had with the true history of slavery and Reconstruction, Du Bois asks, rhetorically: "[A]re these reasons of courtesy and philanthropy sufficient for denying Truth?"[9] The story of the fight to preserve the innocence of white American children and justify American racial hierarchies *is* US history. These efforts, once imagined to be a relic of the past, have come alive again, fueling the ascendant fascist political movements that inspired this book.

Some educational book publishers, for instance, have begun to conform to false and misleading narratives pushed by right-wing activists and commentators. A widely distributed series of high school history textbooks issued to Texas students in 2015 identified enslaved Black Americans as "workers."[10] And in 2023, the state of Florida issued new standards for African American history, which called for educators to teach that enslaved Black Americans "developed skills which, in some instances, could be applied for their personal benefit."[11]

Carter Godwin Woodson is most famous today for his introduction of Black History Month. In 1933, Woodson published a now-classic work on the ways American education was failing Black Americans, titled *The Mis-education of the Negro*. In it, Woodson lambastes classical education, commenting that Black people in this system were "given little thought, for the best friends of the race, ill-taught themselves, followed the traditional curricula of the times, which did not take the Negro into consideration except to condemn or pity him."[12] About, for example, the teaching of literature, Woodson noted that in the traditional curriculum Black people were "not supposed to have expressed any thought worth knowing."[13]

The most visible current manifestation of the Black American tradition of reclaiming history is Nikole Hannah-Jones's 1619 Project. While the project's aim is to place the institution of slavery and its legacy at the center of American history, it does not contradict America's greatness. It rather celebrates the contributions Black Americans have played in it. Despite this fact, it elicited a harsh backlash from right-wing politicians and commentators, who criticized it—in many cases without reading it or taking any time to scrutinize the substance of its claims—for advancing a pessimistic view of America that encourages white people to feel ashamed of their history. In his speech in September 2020 at the White House Conference on American History, Donald Trump denounced the project, along with critical race theory, as "toxic propaganda."[14] The 1619 Project has been targeted specifically by some states, such as Florida, prohibiting its teaching in public schools.

Of course, the United States is by no means the only place where marginalized groups have fought back against attempts to erase their history and culture. As we saw in chapter 2, British colonialists in Kenya attempted to dismantle the traditional governing structures of Kikuyu society. Because the British erroneously assumed that all African tribes had chiefs, they appointed some Kikuyu to this role, fundamentally altering a society that was in reality governed by councils of elders. Ultimately, these and other British interventions had a devastating effect on the Kikuyu. But the Kikuyu nevertheless waged a concerted resistance against British attempts to exterminate their identity. With Jomo Kenyatta as its leader, the Kikuyu Central Association was formed in the early 1920s to defend traditional Kikuyu practices and land interests against the British colonizers.

Kenyatta would go on to study with the Polish-British anthropologist Bronisław Malinowski from 1935 to 1938 at the London School of Economics, writing a dissertation titled

Facing Mount Kenya. In this work, he represents the Kikuyu's traditions and practices in detail, showing that they are central to the Kikuyu religion—and, in so doing, making clear that the British efforts to eliminate the Kikuyu religion were tantamount to the elimination of Kikuyu identity. *Facing Mount Kenya* was written to educate multiple audiences, inside and outside Kenya, and ultimately became an internationally resonant work that aided the African nationalist struggle against European colonialism. It also was a detailed record of the traditions and practices of the Kikuyu religion and way of life, left to future generations of Kenyans.[15]

✦   ✦   ✦

Authoritarian governments are well aware of the democratic possibilities of reclaiming history. It is a hallmark of such governments and the political movements that support them to harass and intimidate such projects.

The Invisible Histories Project is an Alabama project that, according to its website, is "[d]esigned to be a repository for the preservation of LGBTQ life first in the state of Alabama and then the entire Southeast." Like Hirschfeld's Institut für Sexualwissenschaft in Berlin, it is set up as an archive that documents LGBTQ lives and perspectives. Also like Hirschfeld's institute in Germany, it became a target for fascist lawmakers. When the Alabama Department of Archives and History invited one of the project's founders to participate in a presentation, politicians in the Alabama State Senate proposed slashing half of the department's budget. When this failed, they proposed replacing their entire board of directors with political appointees under the control of the state's executive and legislative branches, which are dominated by Republicans. In describing this situation in an opinion piece, AL.com columnist Kyle Whitmire writes:

> History in Alabama is under attack again. A handful of state lawmakers are on a mission to erase it, to cancel those who would mention it and punish those who would protect it.
>
> No less than a revered state institution is on the line—the Alabama Department of Archives and History—and the stories it exists to preserve.
>
> But this time it's not stories of Reconstruction or civil rights protests at risk of being lost. At least, not yet. Rather, something more recent.
>
> It's LGBTQ history in lawmakers' crosshairs.[16]

Another instance in which efforts to reclaim history elicited an outsized backlash can be found in the story of the Museum of the Second World War in Poland, which was conceived in 2008 by an international consort of scholars in the Polish city of Gdańsk and opened in 2017. Its goal was to teach the Second World War, situating Poland's experience within a global perspective. Instead of accentuating Poland's victimhood at the expense of every other victim of the Second World War, the museum gave each population that suffered individual treatment—including the Polish Jewish population killed in the Holocaust and the Soviet prisoners of war indiscriminately massacred by the Nazis. In doing so, the museum corrected long-standing omissions in Poland's understanding of its own history, countering claims that the Polish had suffered uniquely.

Poland's right-wing Law and Justice Party, however, found the museum's restoration of these omissions threatening, and persecuted the organization through both the judicial system and the media. Before the museum was opened in 2017, the Law and Justice Party replaced its director, Paweł Machcewicz, and forced it to change its narrative to a more traditional account that emphasizes the uniqueness of Polish suffering during the war. It is no accident that an anti-democratic party targeted this museum. It is a kind of erasure of history that is aimed at erasing liberal democracy.

✦　✦　✦

As we have seen, authoritarian governments characteristically seek to control the past. Russia bans Ukrainian history in order to gather the Russian population's support behind its colonial ambitions. In the United States, as we have seen, organizations like the Heritage Foundation that support attacks on critical race theory also push for more restrictive voting laws. Authoritarian movements advance restrictive education programs and ban perspectives that place an exceptionalist narrative into question.

When scholarship challenges dominant narratives about the past, difficult truths are revealed—about not only history but subsequent efforts to conceal that history as well. For this reason, this sort of critical scholarship is a profound threat to authoritarian movements. As democratic theorists have long celebrated, democracy encourages an open-ended search for truth, and seeks to include new perspectives, narratives, and data that, however painfully, challenge old assumptions.

If we are to stop the United States' drift toward fascism, we must recognize the nature of the challenges facing our educational institutions. Schools and universities are indeed on the front lines of the multi-decade far-right effort to reinforce anti-democratic myths—and, ultimately, to transform a flawed but hopeful liberal democracy into an authoritarian, potentially fascist nation-state.

My father, Manfred Stanley, who like his mother was a refugee from Nazi Germany, became a professor at Syracuse University's Maxwell School of Citizenship and Public Affairs. My father and stepmother, Mary Stanley, also of the Maxwell School, researched, studied, taught, wrote on, and led educational initiatives that explored what a rigorously democratic education demands of educators, members of democratic political communities, and ultimately of elected officials at all levels.

In one of the articles he wrote in his career as a sociologist, my father teased out how a common reality might be possible in an increasingly pluralistic and complex society,[17] pointing to a type of education that might serve as an alternative to the sort described throughout this book. Civic friendship, he notes, is a requirement for a modern political community that takes democratic values seriously: "Civic friendship, remember, is that concept which signifies the underlying equality of regard which all persons are supposed to have for each other as citizens despite their diverse positions in the social division of labor."[18] Civic compassion, too, he explains, is an essential aspect of democratic civic life:

> As the history of Western totalitarianism has taught us, the ultimate test of compassion is civic defense: the stance of citizens towards each other, as civil neighbors, far and wide, who will not abandon people to avoidable suffering, or to murderers. Much less demanding tests are failed. However, before this final test is reached, how may we articulate what is meant sociologically by civic compassion?
>
> When a society evolves into a condition that is so complex and fragmented by social class and occupational specialization that great sociopsychic distance between population groups becomes a normal state of affairs, then insufficient compassion emerges as a distinct, collective, moral problem. In non-democratic

societies, this problem is mitigated by hierarchical corporate status ideologies. In democratic societies, the problem persists, but it's usually defined in terms of the language of "unity," or "solidarity." To suggest that compassion is a better term is not semantic quibbling. The other two terms are too abstract and contaminated by propagandistic usage. Compassion is more concrete and a more reasonable expectation to have of people. Mutual estrangement, and stereotypical fantasy exist between the extremes of our class structure, between several ethnic and racial groups and between considerable numbers of males and females. This presents a major challenge for civic education, but it is not one of inducing some unrealistic and sentimental attitude of "unity." The challenge is the more difficult one of bringing people to the point of understanding the objective historical and existing conditions of groups with whom they have had no personal life experience. Compassion presupposes the ability to "take the role of the other" in some particularly subtle, and informed way.[19]

My father's vision of civic compassion was premised on rejecting the language of unity, as too "contaminated by propagandistic usage." If anything, his solution was the opposite—to engage respectfully, to imaginatively stand in the places of others, to inhabit worlds that initially seem strange and even threatening, to acknowledge one's inability to be as wise, as generous, or as open as pluralistic democracy requires.

To resist the slide into cruelty is perhaps the most important educational goal of a people. What forms of education could be appropriate for such an endeavor? In some ways we have already begun to create them: critical race theory, women and gender studies, queer theory, labor history, disability studies, and other bodies of scholarship that show how social movements can succeed in breaking down obstacles to equality and liberation. Such approaches stand to create a lifelong disposition toward civic compassion, and the agency to act on it. Ironically, it may be that the tentative successes of these endeavors have helped to trigger the authoritarian backlash I have described throughout this book. It wouldn't be the first time that a successful progressive educational movement has provoked a violent countermovement.

So what is to be done now? We could give up on the project of democratic education and resign ourselves to an education system that is incapable of challenging the language and practices of fascism. Or we can continue the struggle, acknowledging that the project of democratic education is both difficult and essential. Fresh scholarship that challenges myths of uniformity makes new approaches to education unavoidable.

Most Americans are already familiar with the hope encapsulated in our national motto, *E pluribus unum*, or "out of many, one." But this project of assimilation has too often served as a means of obscuring perspectives that don't fit our expectations. The United States' function as a melting pot too often asks members of our political community with notable differences to conform to a homogenous ideal. This may have been feasible for a time, but it is not one compatible with a multi-racial democracy, inclusive of many religions and many different ways of life.

My maternal grandparents are from Eastern Poland and in 1940 were deported to the Gulag, along with my aunt and approximately 130,000 other Polish Jews, at Stalin's orders. My mother was born en route. The family spent the next five years in the Siberian Gulag. My grandfather was interned at a men's labor camp; my grandmother, my mother, and my aunt were sent to another camp far away. Of the 130,000 deported, 80,000 were alive in 1945—the largest group of Polish Jews to survive the Holocaust. Before the war, around 10 percent of the entire population of Poland was Jewish, 3.3 million out of a total population of just over 30 million. By the time the Nazis were defeated, they had wiped out 90 percent of the Polish Jewish population.[20] In 1950 there were only 45,000 Polish Jews left in Poland. Today there are fewer than 5,000.[21]

My mother was repatriated back to Poland with my aunt and grandmother in 1945, sent west on the Trans-Siberian Railroad. Entirely by accident, on the lengthy route they were reunited with my grandfather, whom my mother had never met. They arrived as a small family in Warsaw, eager to reconnect with relatives. They soon discovered that they were the only ones left. Their grief was compounded by the vicious reception returning Jews received at the hands of non-Jewish

Poles. My grandfather was visibly Orthodox Jewish; when my mother accompanied him on the street, Poles would lean over and spit in her face. In 1948, my grandfather was beaten almost to death on the streets of Warsaw, saved at the last minute (according to family lore) by a Jewish policeman. The incident was written about in a Yiddish-language paper in the United States and soon thereafter they were sponsored for visas, arriving in New York City that summer.

Poland has a long and rich Jewish history, as well as a long history of anti-Semitism. Today Poland identifies as, and is widely considered to be, a uniformly Catholic country. Both of these legacies have, to a large extent, been erased—the memory of the large Polish Jewish population, and the memory of the hatred that was for centuries directed against them, not by Nazis, but by their fellow Poles.

The Borderland Foundation is devoted to educating Polish youth about Poland's rich multi-cultural heritage, including its Jewish heritage. Its center is located in the town of Sejny in Eastern Poland, eighty-three miles from Jedwabne, a larger town that became infamous, after the publication of Jan Tomasz Gross's *Neighbors: The Destruction of the Jewish Community in Jedwabne, Poland*, as the site of a massacre of Jews by their Polish neighbors in July 1941. In this corner of northeastern Poland there is a dark history of anti-Semitic violence—as there is of violence among Poles and Lithuanians and other groups. In 1991, the Borderland of Arts,

Culture and Nations center was set up, which would eventually include a library, in a building in Sejny that was once, before the Second World War, among the most renowned yeshivas, a great site of Jewish learning located just next to a synagogue.[22] As part of its mission, Borderland maintains the sites of both the synagogue and the Talmudic school as centers of art, music, theater, and learning. In the summer, the Klezmer Orchestra of the Sejny Theatre performs to overflowing audiences in the synagogue. The Borderland music program, led by the accordionist and ethnomusicologist Wojciech Szroeder, trains Polish children to play Jewish music—music infused with Slavic, Roma, and Baltic influences as well. Some of those Polish children have grown up to become klezmer musicians, keeping alive a music tradition many believed had been lost forever. Borderland exists to "practice" the memory of Poland's rich multi-lingual and multi-religious heritage. Its work is a tool to be used against demagogic myths of a pure Polish Catholic past.

A similar effort to "practice memory" can be found in Howard Zinn's 1980 book, *A People's History of the United States*, which was a landmark moment in the teaching of US history.[23] Instead of recounting the country's history as a series of achievements by great men, the European explorers who supposedly discovered America, the first American revolutionaries, and the founding fathers, Zinn broke through to a wide audience by writing in the tradition of "histories from below," telling history from the perspective of those who were oppressed and subjugated by hierarchies, and focusing on social movements and acts of resistance. The book stresses the agency of the enslaved people of America, indigenous groups, poor workers, and women, in the face of violent obstacles.

Zinn's book has attracted the ire of the American right wing ever since, and in recent years has become an explicit target of Donald Trump and the political movement he represents. In his 2020 speech at the White House Conference on American History, Trump denounced Zinn, saying, "Our children are instructed from propaganda tracts, like those of Howard Zinn, that try to make students ashamed of their own history."[24]

The Zinn Education Project is an organization that "promotes and supports the teaching of people's history in classrooms across the country."[25] It provides resources such as teacher study groups, online classes, and a quarterly journal, *Rethinking History*, that provides informational sources on histories that face erasure, including topics such as the Reconstruction era, US indigenous history, the roots of the Black Lives Matter movement, and the Palestinian struggle for liberation. More generally, it provides wide-ranging resources on the history of US social movements. It is deeply involved in the fight to defend progressive education in the United States against far-right attacks, for example by keeping teachers up-to-date on anti-CRT campaigns on school boards.

An organization like the Zinn Education Project is on the front lines of the war to defend progressive education, seeking to preserve the history of resistance against hierarchies of class, race, and gender against those who aim to erase it. It also seeks to call attention to these attacks, and the larger anti-democratic movement of which they are a part. Even in these grim times for democracy, there remains ample room for hope.

❖ ❖ ❖

The American Dream holds that this country is unique in its capacity to reward hard work with prosperity—in America, supposedly any hard-working person can have a good middle-class life. The American Dream is often presented as the result of a system of pure free market capitalism. But the history of labor movements in this country exposes this as a myth. Often in the face of violent reprisals by big business interests, labor organizing secured many of the substantive gains for workers that created the American Dream. It was unions that gave American workers the eight-hour workday, the weekend, and a living wage. Unions delivered a package that once allowed autoworkers in Michigan to enjoy a life with leisure time to spend with their families, and money to enjoy it. Despite the many setbacks they have faced in recent decades, American unions can do this again. The leftist socialist ideal of workers uniting is not inimical to America's ethos, but an essential part of it.

Labor history is only one of the many perspectives that challenges American fascist myths. In Black studies, Latin American studies, and indigenous studies, students and teachers confront a story of America that is inconsistent with the myths of national innocence and national purity. Students learn from women's studies courses that history is not just the history of men, and from queer studies that it is not just the history of the straight and cisgendered.

Exposing a nation's citizens to the complex history of its past is not just a form of protection against fascists and demagogues. It is also, as my father would say, an essential prerequisite for civic compassion. Democracy requires a common shared reality, including a common understanding of the past. Civic compassion furthers that understanding. To cite again from my father's quotation above, "[t]he challenge is the more difficult one of bringing people to the point of understanding the objective historical and existing conditions of groups with whom they have had no personal life experience." Without such an understanding, one cedes power to hierarchy, or potentially an autocrat.

Democracy is an ideal. It is an ideal in which every citizen has political equality rooted in the recognition of all people's full humanity. And realizing the ideal of political equality is impossible without an understanding of who has been denied it and why.

No one thinks that Russia's election in 2024 was free. The people of Russia have been lied to. Their acceptance of these lies is not *accidental* to their unfreedom. Their acceptance of these lies *constitutes* their unfreedom. Ignorance too hinders free, informed action. Without knowledge, we cannot act. Battles over education are battles over freedom.

Living in a democracy means considering replacing traditions with new ones. Education in a democracy is an exercise for agency, for self-rule. And part of an ethic of self-rule is a refusal to be ruled by the dead. There are no easy answers about how to craft an education for democracy, to give people the liberty to embrace tradition, without shackling them to it. When traditions are inflated and exaggerated, and critical inquiry into them threatens to expose myths that justify power, it gives authoritarians an excuse to crack down on democracy, via its institutions, the schools.

Plato regarded democracy as impossible. Plato knew his authoritarian system must be based on lies. Besides lying, those in power can ban concepts necessary for understanding the world we inhabit, such as structural racism, and institutions, such as the Gulag. They can ban concepts such as human rights or the equality of humankind. They can ban inquiry into human-caused climate change. Those lacking such essential concepts, or knowledge of essential facts, will respond differently to events. Unaware of the range of explanations and options, they can easily be manipulated.

When we see progress toward multi-racial democracy receding before our eyes, it is easy to become disheartened. A moral of this book is that we have been through this before. When we understand the mechanisms by which democracy is attacked, the ways myths and lies are used to justify actions such as wars, and the scapegoating of groups, we can defend against these attacks, and even reverse the tide. This struggle is part of the action of democracy itself. If we weren't having this struggle, we wouldn't be living in a democracy.

Authoritarianism thrives off inequality and myths that support it. Monarchy survived by a myth of divine selection. Dictatorships survive on the myth that one single leader defines and embodies the nation. Fascism survives off myths that create an outgroup, who are relegated to second-class citizenship, at best. Schools and universities allow for critical inquiry into these myths, and so attacks on them are always the canaries in the coal mine of authoritarianism. There is a reason why there are no American-style liberal arts colleges in authoritarian countries.

It is easy not to be invested in colleges and universities,

especially when their expense has skyrocketed as state investment in them shrinks (almost as if it were planned). But eliminating knowledge and critical inquiry restricts our range of actions. If we do not know about the racial wealth gap, or human-caused climate change, we cannot act to address them.

Authoritarianism must always at some point face reality. Social protest movements have traditionally been an engine by which the people try to make those in power see reality. Participating in these movements is an exercise of democracy. Cracking down on them is an exercise of authoritarianism. As long as there is reality, this cycle will continue. New technology, such as Artificial Intelligence (AI), will give it new forms. Misrepresentations and lies spread by AI-based deepfakes are already affecting elections in unpredictable ways, ensuring that voting will proceed in an atmosphere of confusion and ignorance.[1] The protection of democracy requires measures that will ensure people's continued ability to distinguish between true and false.

In countries without a reliable press, such as Myanmar, the confluence of social media misinformation about local events meets with a population that cannot easily fact-check it. The result is disastrous. What is needed to stave off the impending collapse of the information space required for a democracy are honest and fearless teachers and investigative journalists. That's why authoritarians target both.

As I write this epilogue, I am heading to Ukraine, where I am lecturing on this book to university students at the Kyiv School of Economics. Ukrainians are in an existential fight defending their fledgling democracy from an outside fascist threat. In our class, we will discuss the ways in which Ukraine can emerge with a healthy democratic educational system as a fundamental support for their democracy, rather than as a means to create myths of national greatness and national innocence. We will compare their misrepresentation in Russia's educational system to other colonial situations. I expect the discussions to be contentious and productive. The stakes are high, both on the battlefield, for their survival as a nation, and in their press and schools, for their survival as a democracy.

The Russia-Ukraine war is a perfect example of the fact that the fight against fascism is also a fight against fake history. Russian textbooks represent Ukrainians as having no independent historical identity (including no history of genocide), and no distinctive culture or language. They represent the invasion of Ukraine as justified by multiple falsehoods; that Ukrainians are fascists, that the Russians are helping insurgent movements inside Ukraine, and so on. Without these misrepresentations, Russians would not support this war. It is in schools and universities where this fake history is fought. That's why I am headed to Ukraine to teach in one.

This book has also been written on the eve of an American election, one that threatens to plunge my own country into authoritarianism, seemingly willingly, without an external fascist regime such as Russia to threaten us. The authoritarian movement has fought a multi-front war against American democracy. Schools, the press, and political opponents have been tarred as anti-American. Labor rights, climate change action, and women's rights have been restricted in the name of supposedly American values (capitalism and Christianity). The next phase is to attack democracy itself with the same charge. It is up to the rest of us to define a different version of America, one that is conducive to democracy and human flourishing and that justifies a role in the world as an example, not a warning.

In these pages, I have tried to do honor to the multiple legacies of my children, who are the direct descendants of enslaved Black Americans, Kikuyu, and survivors of the Holocaust, drawing from each of the intellectual traditions that intersect with these experiences. The bonds of family and friendship are my own foundational supports. They are a base to build mutual recognition of the fact that we are, in the end, all part of the same human family.

ACKNOWLEDGMENTS

As should be clear throughout, this book is written as an extension of the work of my father, Manfred Stanley, who passed away in 2004. I owe a large debt to him. I inherit from Sara Stanley, my mother, the tenacity to finish my projects (and in case I forget, she reminds me every day that a project not completed is one that in some sense was never started). My mother and father's lived experiences through the trauma of Nazism and Stalinism have also shaped this book in obvious ways. My stepmother, Mary Stanley, has been an immense intellectual influence on me over the decades. She has read and commented on everything I have written lately, including this book. I am indebted to her capacity to channel and transmit to me her intellectual legacy, as well as the sense of responsibility to carry it forward.

I met Tim Snyder in 2015, and we have had an ongoing conversation ever since. These discussions, as well as our jointly taught seminars, have shaped my thinking so deeply that no acknowledgment would be enough.

Kimberlé Crenshaw's work has been pivotal to me. I have learned so much from her decades of thinking and activism on these issues. She is my role model for activism informed by theory, and theory informed by activism.

I am fortunate to have an extraordinary team of friends who are also my Yale colleagues. Marci Shore read some of the earliest drafts of the book, and made crucial interventions. In fact, no other interventions to improve this book have been as dramatic or important as Marci's. In addition to Marci Shore and Tim Snyder, my most frequent interlocutors, the ideas in this book have been aired and tested out in conversations over the years with Jack Balkin, Robin Dembroff, Roderick Ferguson, Elizabeth Hinton, and Tracey Meares. Nothing like this book would have been possible without them. In addition, Ned Blackhawk provided essential help with indigenous American history and discussions about colonialism, and Caleb Smith helped with advice about how to fit my life into my theory. Last and certainly not least, I have learned much from discussions with Chinmayi Arun about topics from India and Myanmar's information spaces to theoretical positions in the philosophy of propaganda.

Other colleagues at Yale have helped me become a scholar who can write about these topics. Mira Debs originally urged me to teach Philosophy of Education, and has been a source of help and insight during my multi-year transition to being a philosopher of education. Naftali Kaminski crucially influenced the parts of this book about Israeli history, as did Eliyahu Stern. During the writing of this book, there were campus protests at Yale. Naftali, Dara Strolovitch, and Gregg Gonsalves helped me the most in thinking through how these protests should inform the broader themes of this book. I am fortunate to have all of these people as colleagues and as friends.

The ideas for this book coalesced in the courses I have taught at Yale, and the theses I have helped advise. I owe a debt to all my students. Among these students, Angel Nwadibia, Taylor Carroll, Sachien Fernando, Carly Benson, and Wren Wolterbeek stand out as those who helped me most specifically with the ideas in this book.

Grace Ellis was not a student of mine, but her advice and background knowledge shaped my discussion of the textbook *American Pageant*.

The course that pulled this book together for the first time was, surprisingly, not taught at Yale. It was a course on colonialism and fascism taught at the Kyiv School of Economics in the summer of 2023, the second summer of Russia's war on Ukraine, in eight consecutive multi-hour lectures (two of which had to be held in a bomb shelter). I'm grateful to the many students who sat in and participated in that course, and chiefly to my teaching assistant, Mariam Naiem.

Colleagues outside of Yale have also been profoundly formative. I am deeply indebted to Susanna Siegel for helping me with my theoretical views of fascism. Benjamin Justice was there from the beginning of my education as a philosopher of education. Ben helped me with my first syllabus in Philosophy of Education five years ago, talked me through the themes of this book before I started it, suggested crucial reading for me, and read and commented on the earliest drafts. David Beaver and I had just completed a book we had been working on for eight years together when I started this one. My work with him has without a doubt influenced this work. Federico Finchelstein has been an invaluable interlocutor and coauthor. He has shaped my thinking about fascism and authoritarianism as much or more than anyone. Discussions with Anthea Butler on white Christian nationalism, and Jarvis Givens on education have been central to my intellectual development. I'm indebted to Henry Giroux's groundbreaking work on critical pedagogy, which has profoundly shaped my thinking over the years. Merve Emre helped me structure my book proposal in vital ways. Finally, Nicole Fleetwood consistently kept my hand to the conceptual and ethical fire through most of the writing of this book, her steel-trap intellect guiding me away from concessions that were true neither to my ethics nor my arguments.

During the writing of the book I hired two research assistants: Tentiana Kotelnykova helped me with Russian textbooks, and Peyton Aiken helped me with American ones. Thanks to them and to Ena Alvarado, who assisted with fact-checking. Karen Thande assisted me with the discussion of Kenya's schools. I'm indebted to Connor Guy's editorial assistance; his contributions at a critical time greatly improved the manuscript.

Much important and largely invisible labor goes into a book's publication. Many thanks to my editor, Nicholas Ciani, whose advocacy and editorial input has been invaluable, and to Julia Cheiffetz, who saw the book's initial promise. I'm deeply grateful for the entire team at One Signal Press who helped bring the project across the finish line and into the world: Alessandra Bastagli, Libby McGuire, Joanna Pinsker, Nicole Bond, Mark LaFlaur, Zakiya Jamal, with special thanks to Hannah Frankel for her ever-steady guidance and support.

My agent, Stephanie Steiker, has been my biggest champion over the years. I put her through a lot during this pressure-filled year because I relied on her the most of anyone. She always and invariably came through.

My two children, Emile and Alain, were a consistent source of joy during the writing of this book, as well as reminders of its importance.

NOTES

Preface

1. Victoria Amelina, "Nothing Bad Has Ever Happened: A Tale of Two Genocides: The Holocaust and the Holodomor," *Irish Times*, May 19, 2022, https://www.irishtimes.com/culture/books/nothing-bad-has-ever-happened-a-tale-of-two-genocides-the-holocaust-and-the-holodomor-1.4879627.

2. Jason Stanley, *How Fascism Works: The Politics of Us and Them* (New York: Penguin Random House, 2018).

3. Henry-Louis de la Grange, *Gustav Mahler*, vol. 2, *Vienna: The Years of Challenge (1897–1904)* (New York: Oxford University Press, 1995), 172–74.

4. See "Ilse Stanley," *This Is Your Life*, November 2, 1955, https://www.youtube.com/watch?v=yYQTBwgGgdw, for a discussion between my grandmother and Fritz Lang about her role in *Metropolis* and how he had known about her (starting at 11:40).

5. Rahel Jaeggi, *Critique of Forms of Life* (Cambridge, MA: Harvard University Press, 2018).

6. Florida Department of Education, *2022-2023 K-12 Social Studies Examples of Rejected Materials*, https://www.fldoe.org/academics/standards/instructional-materials/2223-k12-ss-examples.stml.

1. How to Create an Autocracy

1. Mary Ilyushina, "To please Putin, universities purge liberals and embrace patriots," *Washington Post*, May 7, 2024, https://www.washingtonpost.com/world/2024/05/07/russia-universities-education-putin-overhaul/.

2. Toni Morrison, "Racism and Fascism," in *The Source of Self-Regard: Selected Essays, Speeches, and Meditations* (New York: Alfred A. Knopf, 2019), 14–16.

3. Carl Schmitt, *The Concept of the Political*, expanded ed., trans. George Schwab (Chicago: University of Chicago Press, 2007), 27.

4. Elizabeth F. Cohen, *Semi-Citizenship in Democratic Politics* (Cambridge: Cambridge University Press, 2009).

5. Kimberlé Crenshaw, "Mapping the Margins: Intersectionality, Identity Politics, and Violence against Women of Color," *Stanford Law Review* 43 no. 6 (July 1991): 1241–99.

6. Elizabeth Hinton, *America on Fire: The Untold History of Police Violence and Black Rebellion since the 1960s* (New York: Liveright, 2021), 21.

7. Audre Lorde, "Age, Race, Class, and Sex: Women Redefining Difference," in *Sister Outsider: Essays and Speeches* (Trumansburg, NY: Crossing Press Feminist Series, 1984).

8. See Jill Colvin and Bill Barrow, "Trump's Vow to Only Be a Dictator on 'Day One' Follows Growing Worry over His Authoritarian Rhetoric," APnews.com, December 7, 2023, https://apnews.com/article/trump-hannity-dictator-authoritarian-presidential-election-f27e7e9d7c13fabbe3ae7dd7f1235c72; and Anjali Huynh and Michael Gold, "Trump Says Some Migrants are 'Not People' and Predicts a 'Blood Bath' If He Loses," *New York Times*, https://www.nytimes.com/2024/03/16/us/politics/trump-speech-ohio.html.

9. Peter Stone, "'Openly Authoritarian Campaign': Trump's Threats of Revenge Fuel Alarm," *The Guardian*, November 22, 2023, https://www.theguardian.com/us-news/2023/nov/22/trump-revenge-game-plan-alarm.

10. "Donald J. Trump's Plan to Save American Education and Give Power Back to Parents," January 26, 2023, from the Trump 2024 campaign website, https://www.donaldjtrump.com/agenda47/president-trumps-plan-to-save-american-education-and-give-power-back-to-parents.

11. American Association of University Professors, *Report of a Special Committee: Political Interference and Academic Freedom in Florida's Public Higher Education System*, https://www.aaup.org/report/report-special-committee-political-interference-and-academic-freedom-florida%E2%80%99s-public-higher.

12. Lisa Pine, *Education in Nazi Germany* (London: Bloomsbury, 2010), 42.

13. Elizabeth A. Harris and Alexandra Alter, "Book Bans Are Rising Sharply in Public Libraries," *New York Times*, September 21, 2023, https://www.nytimes.com/2023/09/21/books/book-ban-rise-libraries.html.

14. "Putin Signs Law Expanding Russia's Rules against 'LGBT Propaganda,'" Reuters, December 5, 2022, https://www.reuters.com/world/europe/putin-signs-law-expanding-russias-rules-against-lgbt-propaganda-2022-12-05/.

15. "Extracts from Putin's Speech at Annexation Ceremony," Reuters, September 30, 2022, https://www.reuters.com/world/extracts-putins-speech-annexation-ceremony-2022-09-30/.

16. Heron Greenesmith, "2023 Was the Year of Anti-trans Hysteria," *In These Times*, December 4, 2023, https://inthesetimes.com/article/nashville-tennessee-anti-transgender-hysteria-legislation-attacks-lgbtq.

17. Katalin Madácsi-Laube, "A New Era of Greatness: Hungary's New Core Curriculum," Cultures of History Forum, June 28, 2020, https://www.cultures-of-history.uni-jena.de/politics/a-new-era-of-greatness-hungarys-new-core-curriculum#part4.

18. Nick Thorpe, "Hungary's New Patriotic Education Meets Resistance," BBC.com, February 24, 2020, https://www.bbc.com/news/world-europe-51612549.

19. David P. Goldman, "Fascist Lit and Hungary's Future: L'affaire Nyírő" *Tablet Magazine*, April 16, 2020, https://www.tabletmag.com/sections/arts-letters/articles/hungary-viktor-or-ban-anti-semitism.

20. https://hungarytoday.hu/ministry-of-education-interior-ministry-new-hungarian-orban-ministry/.

21. Megan Brenan, "Americans' Confidence in Higher Education Down Sharply," Gallup.com, "Education" section, (July 11, 2023), https://news.gallup.com/poll/508352/americans-confidence-higher-education-down-sharply.aspx.

22. Anna Ceballos and Sommer Brugal, "Some Teachers Alarmed by Florida Civics Training Approach on Religion, Slavery," *Tampa Bay Times*, June 28, 2022, https://www.tampabay.com/news/florida-politics/2022/06/28/some-teachers-alarmed-by-florida-civics-training-approach-on-religion-slavery/.

23. https://www.foxnews.com/media/greg-gutfeld-you-know-we-got-problems-when-ayatollah-politicians-academia-all-sound-alike. Thanks to Elizabeth Hinton for bringing this clip to my attention.

24. For a remarkable account of the fascist attack on India's universities, see Rahul Bhatia, *The New India: Modi, Nationalism, and the Unmaking of the World's Largest Democracy* (New York: Public Affairs, 2024).

25. https://time.com/6269349/india-textbook-changes-controversy-hindu-nationalism/.

26. https://henryjacksonsociety.org/wp-content/uploads/2021/03/Impact-SE.-Turkey-Erdogan.-JM.pdf.

27. "The Black Teacher Archive Launches at Harvard University," https://www.youtube.com/watch?v=tfibFyXVT3E.

2. Colonizing the Mind

1. W. E. B. Du Bois, "The White Masters of the World," in *The World and Africa* [and] *Color and Democracy*, 11–27 (Oxford: Oxford University Press, 2007), 23.

2. Ngũgĩ wa Thiong'o, *Decolonizing the Mind: The Politics of Language in African Literature* (London: James Curry Press, 1986).

3. Caroline Elkins, *Imperial Reckoning: The Untold Story of Britain's Gulag in Kenya* (New York: Henry Holt, 2005).

4. Ibid., 18–19.

5. Ngũgĩ wa Thiong'o, *Decolonizing the Mind* (Harare, Zimbabwe: Zimbabwe Publishing House, 1981), 3.

6. Ngũgĩ wa Thiong'o, *Birth of a Dream Weaver: A Writer's Awakening* (New York: New Press, 2016), 25.

7. Thiong'o, *Decolonizing the Mind*, 9.

8. Aimé Césaire, *Discourse on Colonialism*, trans. Joan Pinkham (New York: Monthly Review Press, 1972), 14.

9. Timothy Snyder, *Black Earth: Holocaust as History and Warning* (New York: Tim Duggan Books, 2015).

10. Lisa Pine, *Education in Nazi Germany* (London: Bloomsbury, 2010), 48–49.

11. Elkins, *Imperial Reckoning*, 107.

12. Manfred Stanley, Field Notes (unpublished manuscript).

13. David Wallace Adams, *Education for Extinction: American Indians and the Boarding School Experience, 1875–1928* (Lawrence: Kansas University Press, 1995), 184.

14. Ibid., 280.

15. Charles Augustus Goodrich, *The Child's History of the United States: Designed as a First Book of History for Schools* (Philadelphia: Thomas Cowperthwait, 1852), 19–20.

16. Ibid., 281.

17. "History," Hampton University website, https://home.hamptonu.edu/about/history/.

18. Gary Okihiro, *Island World: A History of Hawai'i and the United States* (Berkeley: University of California Press, 2008), 100.

19. Matthew Frye Jacobson, *Barbarian Virtues: The United States Encounters Foreign People at Home and Abroad* (New York: Hill and Wang, 2000), 250.

20. Okihiro quotes Booker T. Washington as saying, "My race in this country can never cease to be grateful to General Armstrong for all that he did for my people and for American civilization. We always felt that many of the ideas and much of the inspiration he used to such good effect in this country, he got in Hawaii." Okihiro, *Island World*, 117.

21. W. E. B. Du Bois, *The Souls of Black Folk* (Chicago: A. C. McClurg, 1903).

22. According to a CBS News article, the publisher claims that 5 million students per year use this textbook. Jericka Duncan, Shannon Luibrand, and Christopher Zawistowski, "Map in Widely Used US History Textbook Refers to Enslaved Africans as 'Immigrants,'" *CBS Mornings*, February 19, 2020, https://www.cbsnews.com/news/the-american-pageant-map-in-widely-used-us-history-textbook-refers-to-enslaved-africans-as-immigrants-cbs-news/.

23. Thomas A. Bailey and David M. Kennedy, *The American Pageant: A History of the Republic*, 7th ed. (Lexington, MA: D. C. Heath, 1983), 2.

24. Subsequent editions of this textbook dropped the wildly misleading statistic about the indigenous population during the time

of European colonization. I am grateful to unpublished work by Grace Ellis, an undergraduate student in American Studies at Yale, in particular "Revising the American Pageant: These Historians Are Gone but Their Influence Is Not" (unpublished paper, Yale College, December 2023).

25. David Ben-Gurion, quoted in Raz Kletter, *Just Past?: The Making of Israeli Archeology* (2006; repr., New York: Routledge, 2014), 46.

26. Noga Kadman, *Erased from Space and Consciousness: Israel and the Depopulated Palestinian Villages of 1948* (Bloomington: Indiana University Press, 2015), 40.

27. Kletter says the count depends on the definition of "village." Kletter, *Just Past?*, 43–44.

28. See Kadman, *Erased from Space and Consciousness*, 71.

29. Shree Paradkar, "How Israel's 'Scholasticide' Denies Palestinians Their Past, Present, and Future," *Toronto Star*, January 24, 2024, https://www.thestar.com/news/world/how-israels-scholasticide -denies-palestinians-their-past-present-and-future/article _8f52d77a-b648-11ee-863d-f3411121907b.html.

30. https://www.ohchr.org/en/press-releases/2024/04/un -experts-deeply-concerned-over-scholasticide-gaza.

31. Hannah Arendt, *The Origins of Totalitarianism* (New York: Harcourt Brace, 1951). The title concerns totalitarianism, but the themes, such as anti-Semitism and racism, generally concern fascism.

3. The Nationalist Project

1. Matthew Frye Jacobson, *Barbarian Virtues: The United States Encounters Foreign People at Home and Abroad* (New York: Hill and Wang, 2000), 261.

2. Johann Gottlieb Fichte, *Fichte: Addresses to the German Nation,*

Cambridge Texts in the History of Political Thought, ed. Gregory Moore (Cambridge: Cambridge University Press, 2009), 58.

3. Benedict Anderson, *Imagined Communities: Reflections on the Origin and Spread of Nationalism* (New York: Verso Books, 1983), 46.

4. Isaiah Berlin, "Herder and the Enlightenment," in *The Proper Study of Mankind* (New York: Farrar, Straus and Giroux, 1997), 411–12.

5. Ibid., 359.

6. Ned Blackhawk, *The Rediscovery of America: Native Peoples and the Unmaking of U.S. History* (New Haven, CT: Yale University Press, 2023), 221.

7. "Christopher Columbus: Explorer of the New World," PragerU Kids, YouTube video, 13:02, https://www.youtube.com/watch ?v=ux54IJ06uHg.

8. Bartolomé de las Casas, *A Short Account of the Destruction of the Indies* (1552; repr., New York: Penguin Books, 1992).

9. Thanks to Elizabeth Hinton for bringing this material to my attention.

10. Candace Owens, "A Short History of Slavery," PragerU, 5:35, https://www.prageru.com/video/a-short-history-of-slavery.

11. Ibid.

12. Thomas Maitland Marshall, *American History* (New York: Macmillan, 1936), 458.

13. Ibid.

14. Blackhawk (2023), 223.

15. Hannah Arendt, *The Origins of Totalitarianism* (New York: Harcourt Brace, 1951), 178–79.

16. Christophe Jaffrelot, *Modi's India: Hindu Nationalism and the Rise of Ethnic Democracy* (Princeton, NJ: Princeton University Press, 2021), 169.

17. Ibid., 171.

18. *Politics in India since Independence*, National Council of Educational Research and Training (NCERT), twelfth grade textbook (PDF), 12, https://ncert.nic.in/textbook.php?leps2=1-8.

19. Hadeel S. Abu Hussein, *The Struggle for Land under Israeli Law: An Architecture of Exclusion* (New York: Routledge, 2023).

20. Vladimir Putin, "On the Historical Unity of Russians and Ukrainians," President of Russia website, July 12, 2021, http://en.kremlin.ru/events/president/news/66181.

21. Ibid.

22. Anderson, *Imagined Communities*, 74.

23. V. A. Beldyugin, S. V. Probeigola., and Y. R. Fedorovsky, *History of the Homeland: Lecture Course* (Luhansk: Publishing House of Vasyl'Stus Donetsk National University, 2017). Thanks to Tentiana Kotelnykova for her translation.

24. L. M. Lyashenko, O. V. Volobuev, and Igor Lvovich Andreeve, *History of Russia* for Grade 11, parts 1 and 2, advanced level, from the series *In-Depth*, approved by the Ministry of Education, 2022. Thanks to Tentiana Kotelnykova for her translation.

25. Ibid., 309. Thanks to Tentiana Kotelnykova for her translation.

26. Report on the Rwandan Genocide, Human Rights Watch, accessed April 15, 2024, https://www.hrw.org/reports/1999/rwanda/Geno1-3-04.htm.

27. J. A. Hobson, *Imperialism: A Study* (1902; repr., London: Allen & Unwin, 1954), 10.

28. Ibid., 11.

29. "The army has never been, and I'm sure never will be or can be, a menace to anybody save America's foes, or aught but a source of pride to every good and far-sighted American," from President Theodore Roosevelt, *The Ship of State, by Those at the Helm* (Boston: Ginn, 1903), 27.

30. In her pivotal 2017 work, *Red Famine: Stalin's War on Ukraine* (New York: Doubleday, 2017), the historian Anne Applebaum brought Holodomor to the world's attention.

31. For example: "In 1932–1933, famine occurred in Ukraine, the North Caucasus, the Volga region, Kazakhstan, and other areas of the USSR. It was primarily caused by the new management system (system, not Stalin's order) in rural areas, aggravated by poor harvests. Consequently, the peasants couldn't fulfill the increasing state demands for grain." In M. Yu, *Russian History: The Early 20th Century Essentials*, ed. V. R. Medinsky, tenth-grade textbook, 2nd ed. in PDF format, with contributions from A. V. Shubin, Yu Myagkov, A. Nikiforov, and others, including revisions, illustrations, and maps (Moscow: Education, 2022), 431 pages.

32. This is the subject of Christopher Browning's classic work, *Ordinary Men: Reserve Police Battalion 101 and the Final Solution in Poland* (New York: HarperCollins, 1992).

33. Frantz Fanon, "On Violence," in *The Wretched of the Earth* (1963; repr., New York: Grove Press, 2004), 51.

34. Émile Durkheim, *Moral Education: A Study in the Theory and Application of the Sociology of Education* (New York: Free Press, 1973), 77, first published in French in 1925, based on lectures given in 1902–1903.

4. From Supremacism to Fascism

1. Adolf Hitler, *Mein Kampf* (New York: Houghton Mifflin, 1971), 288.

2. Ibid., 414.

3. George L. Mosse, "Race and Sexuality: The Role of the Outsider," *Nationalism and Sexuality: Middle-Class Morality and Sexual Norms in Modern Europe*, 140–57 (Madison: University

of Wisconsin Press, 1985), 147. I am grateful to Angelika Kratzer for first directing my attention to the importance of Hirschfeld for understanding that political moment.

4. Brian Puaca, *Learning Democracy: Education Reform in West Germany, 1945–1965* (New York: Berghahn Books, 2009), 20.

5. Lisa Pine, *Education in Nazi Germany* (London: Bloomsbury, 2010), 26.

6. Hitler, *Mein Kampf*, 34.

7. Gilmer W. Blackburn, *Education in the Third Reich: Race and History in Nazi Textbooks* (Albany: State University of New York Press, 1985), preface.

8. Hitler, *Mein Kampf*, 424.

9. Edward Eggleston, *A First Book in American History* (New York: American Book Co., 1889), iii–iv.

10. "Remarks by President Trump at the White House Conference on American History," September 17, 2020, accessed April 15, 2024, https://trumpwhitehouse.archives.gov/briefings-statements /remarks-president-trump-white-house-conference-american -history/.

11. Sarah Churchwell, *Behold, America: The Entangled History of "America First" and "The American Dream"* (New York: Basic Books, 2018).

12. Hitler, *Mein Kampf*, 123.

13. Hitler, *Mein Kampf*, 286. As evidence for this, Hitler appeals to North America's supposed superiority over Central and South America, which he attributes to North America's supposed lack of mixing between its Aryan and non-Aryan populations.

14. "With all his perseverance and dexterity he seizes possession of [the press]. With it he slowly begins to grip and ensnare, to guide and to push all public life, since he is in a position to create and direct that power which, under the name of 'public opinion', is better known today than a few decades ago." Hitler, *Mein Kampf*, 315.

15. Hitler, *Mein Kampf*, 325.

16. Greg Grandin, "Slavery, and American Racism, Were Born in Genocide," *The Nation*, January 20, 2020.

17. The President's Advisory 1776 Commission, *The 1776 Report*, January 2021, https://trumpwhitehouse.archives.gov/wp-content/uploads/2021/01/The-Presidents-Advisory-1776-Commission-Final-Report.pdf.

18. Ibid.

19. Jorge Renaud, "Eight Keys to Mercy: How to Shorten Prison Sentences," Prison Policy Initiative, November 2018, https://www.prisonpolicy.org/reports/longsentences.html.

20. Wendy Sawyer and Peter Wagner, "Mass Incarceration: The Whole Pie 2024," Prison Policy Initiative, March 14, 2024, https://www.prisonpolicy.org/reports/pie2024.html.

21. Ibid.

22. Emily Widra and Tiana Herring, "States of Incarceration: The Global Context 2021," Prison Policy Initiative, September 2021, https://www.prisonpolicy.org/global/2021.html.

23. Sam Levine and Andrew Witherspoon, "Revealed: Florida Republicans target voter registration groups with thousands in fines," *The Guardian*, July 13, 2023, https://www.theguardian.com/us-news/2023/jul/13/florida-fines-voter-registration-groups.

24. Ian Millhiser, "How America Lost Its Commitment to the Right to Vote," *Vox*, July 21, 2021, https://www.vox.com/22575435/voting-rights-supreme-court-john-roberts-shelby-county-constitution-brnovich-elena-kagan.

25. See, e.g., Jonathan Metzl, *The Protest Psychosis: How Schizophrenia became a Black Disease* (Boston: Beacon Press, 2009).

26. Claudia Koonz, *Mothers in the Fatherland: Women, the Family, and Nazi Politics* (New York: St. Martin's Press, 1968), 48.

27. "Hitler's Speech to the National Socialist Women's League (September 8, 1934)," *German History in Documents and Images*,

German Historical Institute, Washington, DC, https://ghdi .ghi-dc.org/sub_document.cfm?document_id=1557.

28. Victoria de Grazia, *How Fascism Ruled Women: Italy 1922–45* (Berkeley: University of California Press, 1992), 43–44.

29. Nancy MacLean, *Behind the Mask of Chivalry: The Making of the Second Ku Klux Klan* (New York: Oxford University Press, 1994).

30. Udi Greenberg, "Gender and the Radical Right's Departures from Fascism," reprinted in *Did It Happen Here?: Perspectives on Fascism in America*, ed. Daniel Steinmetz-Jenkins (New York: W. W. Norton, 2024), 298–304.

31. Some democratic political theorists infamously failed to real-ize the centrality of equality, particularly equality between the sexes, to a democratic culture—see the final chapter of Rousseau's *Émile*.

32. Masha Gessen, *The Future Is History: How Totalitarianism Reclaimed Russia* (New York: Riverhead, 2017).

33. American Association of University Professors, *Report of a Spe-cial Committee: Political Interference and Academic Freedom in Florida's Public Higher Education System*, December 2023, https: //www.aaup.org/file/AAUP_Florida_final.pdf.

34. Movement Advancement Project, "Under Fire: Erasing LGBTQ People from Schools and Public Life, Movement," March 2023, https://www.mapresearch.org/file/MAP-Under-Fire-Erasing -LGBTQ-People_2023.pdf.

35. Patricia Mazzei, "Legal Settlement Clarifies Reach of Florida's 'Don't Say Gay' Law," *New York Times*, March 11, 2024, https: //www.nytimes.com/2024/03/11/us/florida-dont-say-gay-law -settlement.html.

36. Thanks to Elena Kostuchenko for discussion here.

37. "The American Left: From Liberalism to Despotism," Hillsdale College, https://online.hillsdale.edu/landing/american-left.

38. Moira Weigel, "Hating Theory: 'Cultural Marxism,' 'CRT,' and the Power of Media Affects," *International Journal of Communication* 17 (2023): 6504–24.

5. Anti-education

1. From Tom Cotton tweet on X, January 2, 2024, accessed April 15, 2024, https://twitter.com/TomCottonAR/status/1742271 547493019657.
2. "'Somehow She's the Victim?': DeSantis Lays In to Claudine Gay After Resignation As Harvard President," *Forbes Breaking News* on YouTube, https://www.youtube.com/watch?v=Scnt-_u GQLA.
3. Ted Cruz, *Unwoke: How to Defeat Cultural Marxism in America* (Washington, DC: Regnery, 2023).
4. See Education page on website of Congresswoman Elise Stefanik, https://stefanik.house.gov/education.
5. Convention on the Prevention and Punishment of the Crime of Genocide, https://www.un.org/en/genocideprevention/documents /atrocity-crimes/Doc.1_Convention%20on%20the%20 Prevention%20and%20Punishment%20of%20the% 20Crime%20of%20Genocide.pdf.
6. Gilder Lehrman Institute of American History, "Ronald Reagan on the unrest on college campuses, 1967," https://www.gilder lehrman.org/history-resources/spotlight-primary-source/ronald -reagan-unrest-college-campuses-1967.
7. Gilder Lehrman Institute of American History, https://www .gilderlehrman.org/sites/default/files/content-images/04929p1 .web_.jpg.
8. Stephanie Saul, Alan Blinder, Anemona Hartocollis, and Maureen Farrell, "Penn's Leadership Resigns amid Controversies over Antisemitism," *New York Times*, December 9, 2023, https:

//www.nytimes.com/2023/12/09/us/university-of-penn
sylvania-president-resigns.html.

9. Reeves Weideman, "Raging Bill," *New York Magazine*, February
12, 2024, https://nymag.com/intelligencer/article/bill-ackman
-war-harvard-mit-dei-claudine-gay.html.

10. Elise Stefanik, "Statement on Long Overdue Resignation of
Harvard President," January 2, 2024, https://stefanik.house
.gov/2024/1/statement-on-long-overdue-resignation-of
-harvard-president.

11. Harvard University faculty page of Dean Claudine Gay, accessed April 15, 2024, https://facultyresources.fas.harvard.edu
/claudine-gay-1.

12. John McWhorter, "We Need a New Word for 'Plagiarism,'" *New
York Times*, January 23, 2024, https://www.nytimes.com/2024
/01/23/opinion/plagiarism-claudine-gay-ackman-oxman.html.

13. See Ian Ward interview with Christopher Rufo, *Politico*, January 3,
2024, https://www.politico.com/news/magazine/2024/01/03
/christopher-rufo-claudine-gay-harvard-resignation-00133618.

14. Sameer Yasir, "'It Is Suffocating': A Top Liberal University Is
under Attack in India," *New York Times*, February 10, 2024,
https://www.nytimes.com/2024/02/10/world/asia/india-bjp
-jnu.html.

15. Geeta Pandey, "Pinjra Tod: Freed India activists talk about hope
and despair in jail," BBC.com, June 29, 2021, https://www.bbc
.com/news/world-asia-india-57648106.

16. Shreya Basak, "Revisiting Pratap Bhanu Mehta's Resignation
As Ashoka University Faces Heat over Electoral Manipulation
Paper," *Outlook*, August 11, 2023, https://www.outlookindia.com
/national/revisiting-pratap-bhanu-mehta-s-resignation-as
-ashoka-university-faces-heat-over-electoral-manipulation
-paper-news-309791.

17. Yasir, "'It Is Suffocating.'"

18. Karen Fischer, "A Playbook for Knocking Down Higher Ed," *Chronicle of Higher Education*, October 18, 2022, https://www.chronicle.com/article/a-playbook-for-knocking-down-higher-ed.

19. Henry Reichman, "The Professors Are the Enemy," https://www.chronicle.com/article/the-professors-are-the-enemy?sra=true.

20. Theodoric Meyer, Maggie Severns, and Meredith McGraw, "'The Tea Party to the 10ᵗʰ Power': Trumpworld Bets Big on Critical Race Theory," *Politico*, June 23, 2021, https://www.politico.com/news/2021/06/23/trumpworld-critical-race-theory-495712.

21. Project 2025, "180-Day Playbook," https://www.project2025.org/playbook/.

22. Michael Kruse, "DeSantis' Culture Warrior: 'We Are Now over the Walls,'" *Politico*, March 24, 2023, https://www.politico.com/news/magazine/2023/03/24/chris-rufo-desantis-anti-woke-00088578.

23. American Association of University Professors, *Report of a Special Committee: Political Interference and Academic Freedom in Florida's Public Higher Education System*, December 2023, https://www.aaup.org/report/report-special-committee-political-interference-and-academic-freedom-florida%E2%80%99s-public-higher.

24. Ibid.

25. Ibid.

26. It is thus hypocritical in the extreme for the forces connected to DeSantis to launch defenses of "meritocracy" for decisions about university presidencies, given what is occurring under DeSantis.

27. The DeVos family has been engaged in a "decades long effort to direct taxpayer dollars to private schools." See Koby Levin and Tracie Mauriello, "DeVos-Funded Campaign for School Voucher–like plan Withdraws Petitions in a Sign of Defeat," Chalkbeat,

January 9, 2023, https://www.chalkbeat.org/detroit/2023/1/9/23547548/michigan-devos-school-choice-private-schools-petitions-withdrawn-let-mi-kids-learn/.

28. Noam Scheiber, "Betsy DeVos, Trump's Education Pick, Plays Hardball with Her Wealth," *New York Times*, January 7, 2017, https://www.nytimes.com/2017/01/09/us/politics/betsy-devos-education-secretary.html.

29. Andy Kroll, "Behind Michigan's 'Financial Martial Law': Corporations and Right-Wing Billionaires," *Mother Jones*, March 23, 2011, https://www.motherjones.com/%20politics/2011/03/michigan-snyder-mackinac-center/.

30. Anna Clark, "Michigan Still Allows Emergency Takeovers of Local Governments," ProPublica, July 11, 2023, https://www.propublica.org/article/michigan-emergency-takeovers-flint-detroit.

31. Matt Apuzzo, "Blackwater Guards Found Guilty in 2007 Iraq Killings," *New York Times*, October 22, 2014, https://www.nytimes.com/2014/10/23/us/blackwater-verdict.html.

32. Jon Schwarz, "Erik Prince Calls for U.S. to Colonize Africa and Latin America," The Intercept, February 10, 2024, https://theintercept.com/2024/02/10/erik-prince-off-leash-imperialism-colonialism/.

33. Melinda Cooper, *Family Values: Between Neoliberalism and the New Social Conservatism* (New York: Zone Books, 2017).

34. Ibid., 72.

6. Classical Education

1. W. E. B. Du Bois, *The Souls of Black Folk* (Chicago, A. C. McClurg & Co., 1903), p. 55 .

2. Toni Morrison, "Unspeakable Things Unspoken: The Afro-American Presence in American Literature," in *The Source of*

Self-Regard: Selected Essays, Speeches, and Meditations (New York: Alfred A. Knopf, 2020), 169.

3. Aristotle, *Politics*, book 1, part 5.

4. LaToya Baldwin Clark persuasively argues that the central purpose of the anti-CRT laws in the United States is to preserve white innocence—and uses this to connect it to the "Parent's Rights" movement. See LaToya Baldwin Clark, "The Critical Racialization of Parents' Rights," *Yale Law Journal* 113 (2023): 3003–66.

5. Adolf Hitler, *Mein Kampf* (New York: Houghton Mifflin, 1971), 423.

6. George L. Mosse, *The Crisis of German Ideology: Intellectual Origins of the Third Reich* (1964; repr., Madison: University of Wisconsin Press, 2021), 71.

7. See course listings on Hillsdale College's website, https://online.hillsdale.edu/course-list.

8. See video trailer for American Civilization and Its Decline, a course offered by Hillsdale College, https://online.hillsdale.edu/landing/american-citizenship-and-its-decline.

9. On the civilized savagism paradigm, see David Wallace Adams's *Education for Extinction: American Indians and the Boarding School Experience, 1875–1928* (Lawrence: Kansas University Press, 1975) and my prior discussion of it in chapter 2.

10. Plato, *Republic*, in *Plato: Collected Works*, ed. John M. Cooper (Indianapolis: Hackett, 1997), 971–1223.

11. See Daniel HoSang and Joseph Lowndes, *Producers, Parasites, Patriots: Race and the New Right-Wing Politics of Precarity* (Minnesota: University of Minnesota Press, 2019).

12. Nikolaus Wachsmann, *KL: A History of the Nazi Concentration Camps* (New York: Farrar, Straus and Giroux, 2015), 243.

13. Plato, *Republic*, 338c.

14. Thucydides, *The History of the Peloponnesian War* (New York: Penguin Books, 1988), book 2, chapter 6.

15. Ibid., book 3, chapter 4.

16. Dangerous Speech Project, *Dangerous Speech: A Practical Guide*, April 19, 2021, https://dangerousspeech.org/guide/.

17. "And then, as the children are born, they'll be taken over by the officials appointed for the purpose, who may be either men or women or both, since our offices are open to both sexes." Plato, *Republic*, 460b.

18. Plato, *Symposium*, in *Plato: Collected Works*, 457–505.

19. Toni Morrison, "Black Matter(s)," in *The Source of Self-Regard*, 147.

20. Charles W. Mills, *The Racial Contract* (Ithaca, NY: Cornell University Press, 1997), 59–60.

21. Nicole R. Fleetwood, *Marking Time: Art in the Age of Mass Incarceration* (Cambridge, MA: Harvard University Press, 2020), 29.

22. Mills, *The Racial Contract*.

23. Markovits made this point in discussion in a Yale Legal Theory seminar with the philosopher Emmalon Davis, in November 2023.

24. Louise Antony, "The Importance of Being Partial: The Constructive Role of Bias in Human Life," *The Amherst Lecture in Philosophy* 15 (2022): 3, https://www.amherstlecture.org/antony2022/antony2022_ALP.pdf.

25. In chapter 7 of David Beaver and Jason Stanley, *The Politics of Language* (Princeton, NJ: Princeton University Press, 2023), we argue that the ideal of neutrality is incoherent.

26. Charles Mills, "Black Radical Kantianism," *Res Philosophica* 95.1 (January 2018): pp. 1-33.

27. Alasdair MacIntyre, *Whose Justice? Which Rationality?* (Notre Dame, IN: University of Notre Dame Press, 1988).

7. Reclaiming History

1. Memorial was awarded the Nobel Peace Prize in 2022, https://www.nobelprize.org/prizes/peace/2022/memorial/facts/.

2. See Andrew Higgins, "He Found One of Stalin's Mass Graves. Now He's in Jail," *New York Times*, April 27, 2020, https://www.nytimes.com/2020/04/27/world/europe/russia-historian-stalin-mass-graves.html; and Alexander Marrow and Anton Kolodyazhnyy, "Russian Court Extends Jail Term for Gulag Historian to 15 Years," Reuters, December 27, 2021, https://www.reuters.com/world/europe/russian-court-extends-jail-term-gulag-historian-15-years-2021-12-27/.

3. James W. C. Pennington, *A Text Book of the Origin and History, &c. &c. of the Colored People* (Hartford, CT: L. Skinner, 1841).

4. *Anton Wilhelm Amo's Philosophical Dissertations on Mind and Body*, ed. Stephen Menn and Justin E. H. Smith (Oxford: Oxford University Press, 2022).

5. Jarvis Givens, *Fugitive Pedagogy: Carter G. Woodson and the Art of Black Teaching* (Cambridge: Harvard University Press, 2023), p. 127.

6. A quote Du Bois attributes to a Mr. Woodward, in his book *Meet General Grant*, on p. 716 of *Black Reconstruction in America* (1935; repr., New York: The Free Press, 1992).

7. Du Bois, *Black Reconstruction in America*, 121.

8. "Baltimore mayor faces racist attacks after bridge collapse," NPR, April 4, 2024, https://www.npr.org/2024/04/04/1242294070/baltimore-key-bridge-mayor-brandon-scott-racist-attacks.

9. Du Bois, *Black Reconstruction in America*, 714.

10. Manny Fernandez and Christine Hauser, "Texas Mother Teaches Textbook Company a Lesson on Accuracy," *New York Times*, October 5, 2015, https://www.nytimes.com/2015/10/06/us

/publisher-promises-revisions-after-textbook-refers-to-african
-slaves-as-workers.html?_r=0.

11. Antonio Planas, "New Florida Standards Teach Students That
Some Black People Benefited from Slavery Because It Taught
Useful Skills," NBC News online, July 20, 2023, https://www
.nbcnews.com/news/us-news/new-florida-standards-teach
-black-people-benefited-slavery-taught-usef-rcna95418.

12. Carter Godwin Woodson, *The Mis-education of the Negro* (1933;
repr., New York, Tribeca Books), 17.

13. Ibid., 18.

14. "Remarks by President Trump at the White House Conference on
American History," September 17, 2020, accessed April 15, 2024,
https://trumpwhitehouse.archives.gov/briefings-statements
/remarks-president-trump-white-house-conference-american
-history/.

15. Jomo Kenyatta, *Facing Mount Kenya: The Tribal Life of the
Kikuyu* (London: Secker and Warburg, 1938).

16. Kyle Whitmire, "Alabama Archives Hosted an LGBTQ Speaker.
Now Lawmakers Want the Board Fired," AL.com, January 10,
2024, https://www.al.com/opinion/2024/01/alabama-archives
-hosted-an-lgbtq-speaker-now-lawmakers-want-the-board-fired
.html.

17. Manfred Stanley, "The Mystery of the Commons: On the Indis-
pensability of Civic Rhetoric," *Social Research* 50, no.4 (Winter
1983).

18. Ibid., 871.

19. Ibid., 872–73.

20. See "Murder of the Jews of Poland," Yad Vashem, https://www
.yadvashem.org/holocaust/about/fate-of-jews/poland.html.

21. "Poland," Institute for Jewish Policy Research, https://www.jpr
.org.uk/countries/how-many-jews-in-poland.

22. Magdalena J. Zaborowska, "The Borderland Foundation in

Sejny, Poland," *Journal of the International Institute* 16, no. 2 (Spring 2009), https://quod.lib.umich.edu/j/jii/4750978.0016 .207/—borderland-foundation-in-sejny-poland?rgn=main ;view=fulltext.

23. Howard Zinn, *A People's History of the United States: 1492– Present* (New York: HarperCollins, 1980).
24. "Remarks by President Trump at the White House Conference on American History," National Archives Museum, September 17, 2020, https://trumpwhitehouse.archives.gov/briefings-state ments/remarks-president-trump-white-house-conference -american-history/.
25. "About the Zinn Education Project," Zinn Education Project: Teaching People's History, https://www.zinnedproject.org /about/.

Epilogue

1. Pranshu Verma and Cat Zakrzewski, "AI deepfakes threaten to upend global elections. No one can stop them," *Washington Post*, April 23, 2024, https://www.washingtonpost.com/technology /2024/04/23/ai-deepfake-election-2024-us-india/.

INDEX

A

Abbott, Greg, 50

abortion, Nazis on, 97–98

Ackman, Bill, 115

Adams, David Wallace, 35–36

Addresses to the German Nation (Fichte), 45–46

African Americans. *see* Black Americans

Alabama Department of Archives and History, 172

Alliance High School (Kenya), 30–31

Amelina, Victoria, xi

Amendment 4 (Florida), 94

"America First" movement, 83–84

American Association of University Professors (AAUP), 11–12, 103, 125–26

American Dream, concept and labor history, 182–84

American exceptionalism, 57–58, 66–67, 81–82

American History (textbook), 55–56

American Indian boarding schools, 35–37

"The American Left" course (Hillsdale College), 106–7

American Library Association, 13

The American Pageant (textbook), 39–40, 89

America on Fire (Hinton), 5–6

Amo, Anton Wilhelm, 164

ancient Greece and Rome. *see* classical education

Anderson, Benedict, 46, 63, 73

Anderson, Jessica, 123

anti-colonial nationalism, 47–49, 65–66, 68–73

anti-education, 111–33

    campus anti-war protests, 113–17

    class hierarchy and, 121–23

    goals of, 111, 133

    politicians from elite academic institutions, 111–13, 119–21

    religion and, 117–19

    right-wing libertarianism, neoliberalism, and social conservatism working together against education, 131–33

    Trump administration (2016–20) and Project 2025, 123–31

Anti-Racist Teaching and Learning Collective (ARTLC), 6–7

anti-Semitism. *see also* Nazi Germany

    campus anti-war protests and, 113–17

INDEX

anti-Semitism (*cont.*)
   Great Replacement Theory and, 82–87, 95
   Holocaust and Polish Jews, 178–80
   Holocaust murders outside concentration camps, 70
   in Hungary, 16
   Nazi educational authoritarianism and, 12
   Nazi Germany and assimilated Jews, 84, 105
   Nazi ideology about Aryan race, xiv–xvii, 58, 79, 84–86, 97
   Nazi propaganda on, 79, 108
Antony, Louise, 152
Arendt, Hannah, 33, 43, 58
Aristotle, 135, 139, 142–43, 146
Armstrong, Richard, 37, 39
Armstrong, Samuel Chapman, 37–39
Arrow Cross Party (Hungary), 16
Aryan race, Nazi ideology about, xiv–xvii, 58, 79, 84–86, 97
Ashkenazi Jews, 40–41
Ashoka University (India), 118
assimilation, uniqueness of Americans vs., 177–78
Austin, Sharon Wright, 126–27
authoritarianism
   contemporary social and political movements of, overview, xiii–xiv
   democracy vs., 186
   educational authoritarianism, 12–15
   erasing history by, xi–xxi. *see also* erasing history
   fascism as type of, xii–xiii. *see also* fascism

history revised by. *see* reclaiming history
autocracies, 1–24
   educational authoritarianism of, 12–15
   education and "alien" perspective, 15–24
   education distorted by, 3–9
   fascist culture and, 1–12
   Trump and Project 2025, 9–12

B

Barbarian Virtues (Jacobson), 45
Bauer, Gary, 131
Behold, America (Churchwell), 83
Belgium, 54–55, 65
Bell, Derrick, 4
Benesch, Susan, 145
Ben-Gurion, David, 41
Berlin, Isaiah, 47–48
Bharatiya Janata Party (BJP, India), 59–60, 118
Bharatiya Shiksha Niti Ayog (India), 59
bias
   erasure of events and, 5
   institutional, 101
   "neutrality" example of, 152, 154
   objectivity vs., 152–53
Black Americans
   Black History Month, 169
   Black Lives Matter movement, xxi, 94–95, 108, 181
   civil rights movement, 23, 90
   education and segregationist propaganda, 23
   enslavement of. *see* colonialism; slavery
   Great Replacement Theory and, 82–87, 95

reclaiming history of, 163–71
scholars in elite universities, 162
supremacist nationalism and,
49–57
Reconstruction era (US) and,
55–56
Blackburn, Gilmer W., 80
Blackhawk, Ned, 49, 57
Black Reconstruction in America
(Du Bois), 91, 165–67, 168
Blackwater (military contractor),
130
book banning, 12–15, 75. *see also*
authoritarianism; fascism
Borderland Foundation (Poland),
179
Borderland of Arts, Culture and
Nations (Poland), 179–80
Breivik, Anders, 86
Britain
colonialism in Africa by, 26–37
political elite of, and higher
education, 120
Brown v. Board of Education (1954),
168
Buffalo (New York) supermarket
shootings (2022), 86–87
Bush, George W., 113

C
Caldwell-Stone, Deborah, 13
campus anti-war protests
(1960s, 2023–24), 113–17
Carlson, Allan, 101–2
Cenabre, Marco, 6–7
Central European University
(CEU, Budapest), 17–18, 125
Césaire, Aimé, 32–33
charismatic leaders, of fascist
regimes, 2

China, Tiananmen Square protest/
massacre (1989), xx–xxi
Christians and Christianity. *see*
classical education; religion
Christopher Columbus video
(PragerU), 50–51
Chronicle of Higher Education, 122
Churchwell, Sarah, 83
citizenship. *see also* immigrants
Citizenship Amendment Act
(2019, India), 118
"semi-citizenship," 2–3
United States Reconstruction era
and, 55–56
civic compassion, 174–77
civilization savagism paradigm,
35–37, 47, 49, 140–46, 155
civil rights movement, 23, 90
Civil War, American (1861–65),
53–55, 167
class hierarchy, 121–23. *see also*
anti-education
classical education
for critical thinking, 157
defined, 136
democracy vs. fascism both as
supported by, 146–51
far-right justification of
civilization savagism paradigm
and, 140–46, 155
far-right manipulation of
"Western Values" with, 157–59
as fascist education antidote,
136–37
"neutrality" example of far-right
bias, 152, 154
New College of Florida and, 103
objectivity vs. bias and, 152–53
"Western Canon" and far-right
manipulation of, 137–40

Cleon (Athenian statesman),
144–45
climate change, 66
Cohen, Elizabeth F., 2
colonialism, 25–43. *see also*
nationalism
cultures of hierarchy and, xx–xxi
education systems and, 33–37
identity-based nationalism and,
43
land narratives and, 26–33,
40–43
missionaries and, 37–39
modern colonialism, 25–26
settler colonialism, defined,
39–40
universal vs. non-universal form
of, 47–49
Columbia University, 116–17
Columbus, Christopher, 40, 50–51
Congo, 54–55, 65
conquistadors, 50–53
Conservative Political Action
Conference (CPAC), 16
container ship accident (Francis
Scott Key Bridge, Baltimore,
2024), 167
Coolidge, Calvin, 83
Cooper, Melinda, 131
Corcoran, Richard, 104
Corfield, F. D., 34
Cotton, Tom, 112
counter-Enlightenment, 48
Crenshaw, Kimberlé, 4
critical race theory (CRT), 4–7, 94,
107
critical thinking, 157
Cruz, Ted, 112
"Cultural Marxism," 107, 112. *see
also* Marxism and socialism

culture
"cultural bomb," 30
cultural destruction and
colonialism, 30–33
cultures of hierarchy, xx–xxi
defined, xx

D

Dante, 139
Darwinism, 58, 148
Davidsohn, Magnus, xv–xvi
Davidsohn, Max, xv
Decolonizing the Mind (Thiong'o),
25, 29–30
De Grazia, Victoria, 98–99
democracy, 185–189. *see also*
classical education; hierarchies
authoritarianism vs., 186
classical education in support of
fascism vs., 146–51
flexibility needed for, 185–86
higher education needed for,
187–89
as ideal, 184
liberal democracy, defined, xviii–
xix
perspective recognized by, xi–xii
Department of Education (US),
Trump administration and,
128–31
Department of Justice, US, 123–24
DeSantis, Ron, 19–20, 93, 94,
102–3, 112, 124–27
DeVos, Betsy, 128–30
DeVos, Dick, 128–30
Discourse on Colonialism (Césaire),
32–33
Divine Comedy (Dante), 139
Dmitriev, Yuri, 161–62
"Don't Say Gay" law (Florida), 105

Du Bois, W. E. B., xv, 25, 39, 91, 135, 165–67, 168
Durkheim, Émile, 72

E

education. *see also* anti-education; classical education; nationalism; reclaiming history; *names of individual schools*
"alien" perspective in, 15–24
colonialism and erasing history with. *see* colonialism
educational authoritarianism, 12–15
erasing history with, overview, xi–xiv, xviii, xix–xxi
fascist culture and use of, 1–12, 75–80, 87–90, 97–98, 106–8. *see also* fascism
nationalism and textbooks, 52–53, 55–56, 59–61, 63, 67
Eggleston, Edward, 80–81
Elkins, Caroline, 27–29
Emergency Management Act (Michigan), 129–30
Émile (Rousseau), 149
Enlightenment philosophy, 47–49, 136–37, 146–56
epistemological (knowledge) hierarchy, xix–xx
Erased from Space and Consciousness (Kadman), 41–42
erasing history, xi–xxi. *see also* anti-education; authoritarianism; autocracies; classical education; colonialism; fascism; nationalism; reclaiming history
hierarchies used for, xvii–xxi
history as threatening to authoritarian regimes, xi–xiv

ideology and imposing fictional historical view, xiv–xvii
Russia-Ukraine war as fight against fake history, 188–89
"Erasing LGBTQ People from Schools and Public Life" (2023 report), 104–5
Erdoğan, Recep Tayyip, 22–23

F

Facing Mount Kenya (Kenyatta), 171
family, far-right politicians on, 145–46
Fanon, Frantz, 71
far-right politics. *see* anti-education; classical education; fascism; reclaiming history; religion; Trump, Donald
Fasanenstrasse Synagogue (Berlin, Germany), xiv–xvi
fascism, 75–110. *see also* anti-education
American exceptionalism and, 81–82
anti-leftist education/propaganda of, 106–8
classical education in support of democracy vs., 146–51
cultures of hierarchy and, xx–xxi
defined, xii–xiii
fascist culture and education, 2–12
fascist education on slavery (US), 87–90
fascist education themes, overview, 78
fear and grievance encouraged by, 91–95, 136
gender and "great men" narratives, 80–81, 180–81

fascism (*cont.*)
  gender roles and, 95–101
  Great Replacement Theory,
    82–87, 95
  LGBTQ rights and, 75–76,
    96–97, 100–6
  Nazi educational system and,
    75–80, 97–98
  religion and, 82
  representations and practices in,
    1–2
  Russia-Ukraine war as fight
    against, 188–89
  southern United States, race, and,
    99–100
  supremacist nationalism and,
    109–10
fear, fascism and, 91–95, 136
Fichte, Johann Gottlieb, 45–46,
  63
First Book in American History, A
  (Eggleston), 80–81
Fischer, Karin, 122–23
Fleetwood, Nicole R., 149
Florida
  Black Lives Matter 2020
    uprisings, xxi
  DeSantis and higher education,
    112, 124–27
  fascism and, 93–94
  nationalism and education in,
    50
Ford, Henry, 84
Fox News, 21
Francis Scott Key Bridge (Baltimore),
  container ship accident (2024),
  167
Frankfurt School, 108
Friedman, Milton, 131
Future Is History, The (Gessen), 102

G
Gandhi, Mahatma, 59–61
Gay, Claudine, 114–16, 124
gender and fascism. *see also* LGBTQ
  people
  "great men" narratives and, 80–81,
    180–81
  women's roles and, 95–101
genocide
  cultural, 32, 62
  mass killing and, 86
  United Nations Genocide
    Convention (1948), 113
  university presidents questioned
    about (by US Congress),
    113–17
Germany, World War II–era.
  see Nazi Germany
Gessen, Masha, 101–2
Gibbon, Edward, 138–39
Givens, Jarvis, 23, 164
Gleichschaltung (coordination), 10,
  80
Godse, Nathuram Vinayak, 60
Goebbels, Joseph, 12
Grandin, Greg, 88–89
Grant, Madison, 82–83
"great men" narratives, 80–81,
  180–81
Great Replacement Theory, 82–87,
  95, 108, 109
Greece, ancient. *see* classical
  education
Greenberg, Udi, 100
Greenesmith, Heron, 14
grievance, fascism and, 91–95
Gross, Jan Tomasz, 179
gulags and prisons, 27, 92–93, 178,
  186
Gutfeld, Greg, 21

H

Haiti, 54

Hamas, 20–21, 42, 113–14

Hampton Normal and Agricultural Institute (Virginia), 37–38

Hannah-Jones, Nikole, 169–70

Harvard University, 112–13, 114–16

Hawaii, colonialism in, 37–39

Heidegger, Martin, 157

Herczeg, Ferenc, 16

Herder, Johann Gottfried von, 48, 154–55, 158

Heritage Foundation, 10, 16, 123, 173–74

Heritage of Change (Stanley), 32

hierarchies
  class hierarchy, 121–23. *see also* anti-education
  cultures of, xx–xxi
  segregation and, 2–3. *see also* slavery
  of value vs. epistemology (knowledge), xix–xx

Hillsdale College (Michigan), 19–20, 101–3, 106–7, 138–39

Hindus and Hinduism. *see* religion

Hinton, Elizabeth, 5–6

Hirschfeld, Magnus, 76, 171

history, erasing. *see* erasing history

history, reclaiming. *see* reclaiming history

History of the Decline and Fall of the Roman Empire, The (Gibbon), 138–39

Hitler, Adolf. *see also* Nazi Germany
  conspiracy theories about, 132
  Mein Kampf, 75, 79–81, 84–85, 137

propaganda of, 87, 96–97, 165
  rise to power by, 10, 33

Hobson, J. A., 65–66, 68

Holodomor, 67–68

Horthy, Miklós, 16

House Un-American Activities Committee (HUAC), xvii–xviii

How Fascism Works: The Politics of Us and Them (Stanley), xii

Hume, David, 136, 148

Hungary, education in, 15–19

Hutu people (Rwanda), 65

I

"I Have a Dream" speech (King), 88, 90

"imagined community," 72–73

immigrants
  American First movement and, 83
  representation of, as criminals, 1

Imperialism (Hobson), 65–66

Imperial Reckoning (Elkins), 27–29

India
  education and anti-Muslim laws in, 21–22
  Modi on higher education in, 117–19
  nationalism and, 59–61, 71
  religion of, 82

Institute for Sexual Science (Institut für Sexualwissenschaft), 75–76, 171–72

International Jew, The (Ford's publication), 84

intersectionality, 4

Invisible Histories Project (Alabama), 171–72

Iraq War, Nisour Square Massacre (2007), 130

Islam and Muslims. *see* religion
Israel
    campus anti-war protests and
        (2023–24), 113–117
    Israel-Hamas war and, 20–21,
        42, 113–14
    land disputes in, 40–43
    religion and, 61–62
Italy, fascism and, 85, 98–99,
    100

J
Jacobson, Matthew Frye, 38, 45
Jaeggi, Rahel, xx
Jawaharlal Nehru University (India),
    119
Jefferson, Thomas, 89
Jews and Judaism. *see* anti-Semitism;
    religion
Jim Crow system, 2, 23, 52, 92–94,
    166–68. *see also* Black
    Americans; Reconstruction;
    slavery

K
Kadman, Noga, 41–42
Kalita, Devangana, 117–18
Kamehameha III (Hawaiian king),
    37
Kant, Immanuel, 136, 143, 148,
    149–50
Kenya
    classical education and, 158
    Mau Mau rebellion (1952–60),
        27–34, 47
Kenyatta, Jomo, 170–71
Kertész, Imre, 15–16
Kikuyu (Kenyan ethnic group),
    27–30, 32–34, 170–71

Kikuyu Central Association, 170
King, Martin Luther, Jr., 88, 90,
    142–43
Knesset, 61–62
Koonz, Claudia, 95–96
Kornbluth, Sally, 114
Kroll, Andy, 129
Kruse, Michael, 124–25
Ku Klux Klan (KKK), 56, 83–84,
    99–100, 165–66
Kyiv School of Economics
    (Ukraine), 188

L
labor exploitation, colonialism and,
    37–40. *see also* slavery
labor history, American Dream
    concept vs., 182–84
land. *see* colonialism
language
    colonialism and, 31
    nationalism and, 45–46, 62–64
Las Casas, Bartolomé de, 51
Law and Justice Party (Poland), 173
Leopold II (king of Belgium), 54
Leska, Samm, 7
LGBTQ people
    educational authoritarianism and
        trans rights, 13–15
    "Erasing LGBTQ People from
        Schools and Public Life" (2023
        report), 104–5
    reclaiming history of, 171–72
    rights of, 75–76, 96–97
    as target of fascists, 105–6
liberal arts education. *see* classical
    education
libertarianism
    defined, 121

higher education as target of, 127–33

right-wing libertarianism, neoliberalism, and social conservatism working together against education, 131–33

libraries, book banning and, 12–15, 75. *see also* authoritarianism; fascism

Lincoln, Abraham, 88, 90

Locke, John, 136, 143, 148

Lorde, Audre, 7

M

Machcewicz, Paweł, 173

Mackinac Center for Public Policy (Michigan), 129–130

MacLean, Nancy, 100

Magill, Mary Elizabeth, 114–15

Mahler, Gustav, xv

Malinowski, Bronisław, 170–71

Manhattan Institute, 124

Markovits, Daniel, 151

Marxism and socialism
"Cultural Marxism," 107, 112
fascism on, 77, 106–8
"Marxism" term and, 107
right-wing politicians (US) on elite higher education as, 111–12, 120–21

Massachusetts Institute of Technology (MIT), 114

Mau Mau rebellion (1952–60), 27–34, 47

Maxwell School of Citizenship and Public Affairs (Syracuse University), 174–75

McCarthy, Joseph, 116

McCarthyism (House Un-American Activities Committee, HUAC), xvii–xviii

media
anti-Semitism and, 84
in India, 118
nationalism and, 67
in Poland, 173
in Russia, 67
US anti-war protests and, 20–21

Mehta, Pratap Bhanu, 118

Mein Kampf (Hitler), 75, 79–81, 84–85, 137

Meloni, Giorgia, 100

melting pot concept, uniqueness of Americans vs., 177–78

Memorial (Russian organization), 161–62

Michigan, Emergency Management Act of, 129–30

Mill, John Stuart, 148

Mills, Charles W., 147–48, 151, 156

Mis-education of the Negro, The (Woodson), 169

Mitchell, John, 38

Modi, Narendra, 22, 59, 117

moral personhood concept, 151

Morehouse College (Georgia), 142–43

Morrison, Toni, 1, 8, 135, 147

Mosse, George L., 76, 137–38

Mother Jones magazine, 129

Movement Advancement Project (MAP), 104–5

Museum of the Second World War (Poland), 172–73

Mussolini, Benito, 85

Mytilenean revolt (ancient Greece), 144–45

INDEX

N

Narwal, Natasha, 117–18

National Conservatism Conference (2021), 123

National Council of Educational Research and Training (NCERT, India), 22, 59–60

nationalism, 45–73

  American exceptionalism, 57–58, 66–67

  anti-colonial nationalism, 47–49, 65–66, 68–73

  contemporary social and political movements of, overview, xiii–xiv

  cultures of hierarchy and, xx–xxi

  identity-based, 43

  religion and, 59–62. *see also* religion

  in Russia, 62–64, 67–68

  in Rwanda, 65

  supremacist nationalism, 45–57, 71

National Socialist Women's League (Nazi Party), 96–97

Native Americans, nationalism and, 49–57

Nazi Germany

  Aryan nationalism of, xiv–xvii, 58, 79, 84–86, 97

  classical education and, 137–42, 157

  educational authoritarianism of, 12

  fascism and educational system of, 75–80, 97–98

  fascism and women's roles, 95–96

  Gleichschaltung (coordination) of, 10

  Hungarian nationalism and, 18

  nationalism and language of, 45–46

  nationalism, Holocaust, and post-war German education, 69–70

  racist ideology of, xiv–xvii

  Reich Central Office for the Combating of Homosexuality and Abortion, 98

  Treaty of Versailles and colonialist views of, 33

Ndegwa, Philip, 30

Neighbors (Gross), 179

neoliberalism, anti-education goals of, 131–33

Netanyahu, Benjamin, 61

neutrality (example of far-right bias), 152, 154

New College of Florida, 102–4, 125

"New Woman," 95–96

Nisour Square Massacre (Iraq, 2007), 130

Nixon, Richard, 123

Njonjo, Charles, 30

Nyírő, József, 16

O

objectivity vs. bias, 152–53

Odinga, Jaramogi Oginga, 30

Off Leash with Erik Prince (podcast), 130–31

Orbán, Viktor, 15–19

Origin and History of the Colored People, The (Pennington), 163–164

Origins and Growth of Mau Mau, The (Corfield), 34

Origins of Totalitarianism, The (Arendt), 33, 58

Owens, Candace, 53–55

INDEX

P

Palestinian people, 20, 40–43, 71

Paradkar, Shree, 42

Passing of the Great Race, The (Grant), 82–83

Patterson, Orlando, 147

Peloponnesian War, 144–45

Pennington, James W. C., 163–64

People's History of the United States, A (Zinn), 180–81

Pericles, 143–44

philosophy, classical. *see* classical education; *names of individual philosophers*

Pine, Lisa, 33

Pinjra Tod, 118

Plato, 142–43, 146, 185

"A Playbook for Knocking Down Higher Ed" (Fischer), 122–23

Poland, Holocaust and, 172–73, 178–80

Political Interference and Academic Freedom in Florida's Public Higher Education System report (American Association of University Professors), 125–26

Politico, 116, 123

Politics (Aristotle), 135, 146

poll taxes, 94

"practice memory" concept, 180–82

Prager, Dennis, 50

PragerU, 50–55

Prince, Erik, 130–31

Prison Policy Initiative, 92

prisons and gulags, 27, 92–93, 178, 186

Project 2025, 9–12, 123–31

Putin, Vladimir, 1, 2, 13–14, 62–63, 102, 162

R

Racial Contract, The (Mills), 147–48, 151

"Racism and Fascism" (Morrison), 1

racist ideology. *see also* anti-education; Black Americans; classical education; colonialism; nationalism; Nazi Germany; reclaiming history; slavery

critical race theory (CRT) and, 4–7

fascism in southern United States and, 99–100. *see also* fascism

intersectionality and, 4

Jim Crow system of segregation and, 2

Nazi concept of, 142

of Nazi Germany, xiv–xvii

structural racism, 4–9, 94

Rashtriya Swayamsevak Sangh (RSS, India), 59–60

Reagan, Ronald, 113–14

reclaiming history, 162–84

American Dream, concept and labor history, 182–84

authoritarian concealment as control, 173–74

authoritarian resistance to unflattering history, overview, 161–63

civic compassion needed for, 174–77

defending progressive education for, 182

Holocaust and Poland's history accounts, 172–73, 178–80

reclaiming history (*cont.*)
LGBTQ history revision and, 171–72
"practice memory" concept and, 180–82
racial superiority claims and, 163–71
religious justification of slavery and, 163–64
uniqueness of Americans and, 177–78
Reconstruction (US, 1865–77)
Black Reconstruction in America (Du Bois), 91, 165–67, 168
events during, 55–56
reclaiming history about, 164–68
Rediscovery of America, The (Blackhawk), 49
Red Scare, 1940s–50s (House Un-American Activities Committee, HUAC), xvii–xviii
Reid, Amy, 104
Reinhardt, Max, xv
religion
anti-education and, 117–19
anti-Muslim laws in India, 21–22
Christian fundamentalism/ nationalism in higher education, 19–24
colonialism, "civilization savagism paradigm," and, 35–37
colonialism and dismantling of, 29–34
colonialism and missionaries, 37–38
fascism and, 82

Kikuyu practices, 29. *see also* Kikuyu (Kenyan ethnic group)
nationalism and, 59–62
reclaiming history of slavery and, 163–64
religious narrative about slavery, 163–64
Republic, The (Plato), 142–43, 146
Republican Party (United States). *see* anti-education; classical education; fascism; reclaiming history; Trump, Donald
Rethinking History (journal), 181
Rome, ancient. *see* classical education
Roof, Dylan, 86
Rousseau, Jean-Jacques, 136, 148–49
Rufo, Christopher, 115, 116, 124–25
Russia
fascism and, 101–2
gay propaganda law of, 13
on gender ideology, 14
McCarthyism and, xvii–xviii
nationalism and, 62–64, 67–68
reclaiming history about Stalin, 161–62, 165, 178
2024 election in, 185
Rwanda, 65

S
Schmitt, Carl, 2
Scott, Brandon, 167
Scramble for Africa, 31–33
"semi-citizenship," 2–3
1776 commission, 83, 89–90
Shafik, Minouche, 116–17
Shaheed, Farida, 42

Shelby County v. Holder (2013), 94
Short Account of the Destruction of the Indies, A (Casas), 51
Short History of Slavery, A, video (PragerU), 53–55
1619 Project, 169–70
slavery
  classical education as far-right justification of, 140–51, 155
  far-right higher education on colonialism and, 20. *see also* anti-education; classical education
  fascist education on, 87–90
  reclaiming history about, 163–64, 166–71
  as supremacist nationalism, 49–57
Snyder, Rick, 130
Snyder, Timothy, 33
Socrates, 142, 146
Soviet Union, McCarthyism and, xvii–xviii. *see also* Russia
Spain, nationalism and, 50–51
Stalin, Joseph, 67–68, 161–62, 165, 178
Stanley, Ilse (author's grandmother), xiv–xvi
Stanley, Jason (author), xii
Stanley, Manfred (author's father), 32–34, 75, 138, 158, 174–76
Stanley, Mary (author's stepmother), 174–75
Stefanik, Elise, 112–13, 114–15
structural racism, 4–9, 94. *see also* racist ideology
supremacist nationalism, 45–57
  defined, 46–47
  Enlightenment ideal and, 47–49

  fascism and, 109–10
  language and, 45–46
  slavery as, 49–57
Symposium, The (Plato), 146
Syracuse University, 174–75
Szroeder, Wojciech, 180

T
taxes, 94, 121–22
Texas
  nationalism and education in, 50
  reclaiming history and textbooks of, 168–69
textbooks. *see* education
Thiong'o, Ngũgĩ wa, 25, 29–30, 31, 35
Thirteenth Amendment (United States), 53
Thomson, Judith Jarvis, 153
Thrasymachus, 142, 145
Thucydides, 143–44, 145
Tiananmen Square protest/ massacre (1989), xx–xxi
"tradwife," 100
Treaty of Trianon (1920), 15, 17
Treaty of Versailles (1919), 33, 77, 79
Tree of Life synagogue shootings (2018), 86–87
Trianon, Treaty of (1920), 15
Trump, Donald
  education and, 123–31
  fascism and, 81–82, 87, 89
  nationalism and, 57
  Orbán and, 16
  reclaiming history and, 167, 170, 181
  2024 presidential campaign of, 9–12, 16, 123–31, 188–189

Turkey, education in, 22–23
Tutsi people, 65

U
Ukraine
  Russian nationalism and, 62–64,
    67–68
  Russia-Ukraine war and "gender
    ideology," 14
  Russia-Ukraine war as fight
    against fascism, 188–89
unfreedom, 146–47, 185. *see also*
  classical education
United Kingdom. *see* Britain
United Nations Genocide
  Convention (1948),
  113
United States. *see also* anti-
  education; classical
  education; colonialism;
  education; fascism; nation-
  alism; reclaiming history;
  Reconstruction; slavery; *names
  of individual politicians*
  American exceptionalism, 57–58,
    66–67
  Civil War (1861–65), 53–55
  contemporary interference in
    education, 3–4
  Department of Education, 128–31
  Department of Justice, 123–24
  educational authoritarianism
    and trans rights, 14–15
  HUAC (McCarthyism) in,
    xvii–xviii
  KKK as fascist movement,
    99–100
  Reconstruction era of, 55–56
  right-wing attacks on universities
    in, 18–19

  state laws in, 14–15, 105. *see also
    individual state names*
Thirteenth Amendment, 53
University of Florida, 103
University of Pennsylvania, 114–15
"us" vs. "them"
  "alien" perspective and education,
    15–24
  fascism, defined, xii
  "othering" and, 34, 58
  "semi-citizenship," 2–3

V
value, hierarchy of, xix–xx
Vance, J. D., 112, 123
Versailles, Treaty of (1919), 33
*Virginia: History, Government,
  Geography* textbook (Virginia
  History and Textbook
  Commission), 52–53
Voltaire, 148
voting and elections
  incarceration and, 92–94
  Reconstruction era (US) and, 56
  Russia, 2024 election in, 185
  Trump and 2024 presidential
    campaign, 188–89. *see also*
    Trump, Donald
  voter fraud accusations, 93, 124
  Voting Rights Act (1965), 93–
    94
voucher programs, 20

W
Wachsmann, Nikolaus, 141
Walden, Ruth Terry, 7
Walker, Scott, 122–23
Washington, Booker T., 38–39
Washington, George, 89, 163
Weigel, Moira, 107–8

"Western Values," 157–59
White House Conference on
American History (2020),
81–82, 181
"The White Masters of the World"
(Du Bois), 25
White Replacement Theory, 86–87.
see also Great Replacement
Theory
white supremacy. *see* racist ideology
Whitmire, Kyle, 172
"Whose Country is This?"
(Coolidge), 83
Wilhelm II (German emperor), 77
Williams, Patricia J., 4
Wisconsin, education in, 122–23

Women of the KKK (WKKK),
99–100
women's roles, fascism and, 95–101
Woodson, Carter Godwin, 169
Woodward, W. E., 166
World Congress of Families, 102
World War I
German education system during,
76–77
Treaty of Trianon (1920), 15
Treaty of Versailles (1919), 33
World War II. *see* Nazi Germany

Z
Zinn, Howard, 180–81
Zinn Education Project, 181–82

ABOUT THE AUTHOR

Jason Stanley is the Jacob Urowsky Professor of Philosophy at Yale University. He is the author of six books, including *How Fascism Works* and *How Propaganda Works*. Stanley is a member of the Justice Collaboratory at Yale Law School and serves on the advisory board of the Prison Policy Initiative. He writes frequently about authoritarianism, democracy, propaganda, free speech, and mass incarceration for the *New York Times*, the *Washington Post*, *The Guardian*, *Project Syndicate*, and many other publications.